JOHN: SPIRITUAL THEOLOGIAN

*Now Jesus did many other signs in the presence of his
disciples, which are not written in this book. But these are written so that
you may continue to believe that Jesus is the Messiah, the Son of God, and
that through believing you may have life in his name.*
(Jn 20:30-31)

Wilfrid J. Harrington, O.P.

John: Spiritual Theologian
The Jesus of John

the columba press

First published, 1999, by
the columba press
55A Spruce Avenue, Stillorgan Industrial Park,
Blackrock, Co Dublin

Cover by Bill Bolger
Origination by The Columba Press
Printed in Ireland by Colour Books Ltd, Dublin

ISBN 1 85607 268 1

Contents

Preface

In this series I have, before, looked at the Jesus of Mark, Luke and Matthew.[1] The Jesus of John would seem to be startlingly different. And, in many respects, so he is. Yet, at the end, especially when one takes into account the consistent Johannine emphasis on Jesus as the Sent One, the difference does not loom enormously. The Jesus of Mark and the Jesus of John – the contrast is starkest here – is the one Jesus.

As a scripture scholar one is always beholden to other scholars. I need, in this instance, to acknowledge a special indebtedness to a remarkable recent commentary. It is the work of Francis J. Moloney.[2] A glance at the notes will indicate how much I appreciate his work and how much I have learned from it. With my own commentary on Revelation in the same *Sacra Pagina* series, I am happy to be, in a sense, an associate.

Wilfrid J. Harrington, O.P.

CHAPTER 1

The Fourth Gospel

We declare to you what we have seen and heard so that you also may have fellowship with us; and truly our fellowship is with the Father and with his Son Jesus Christ (1 Jn 1:3)

The problem of the authorship of the fourth gospel is very involved. According to the mainstream of early church tradition, John the Apostle, son of Zebedee and brother of James, wrote, in old age, his gospel in Ephesus. But the tradition is not quite unanimous. And, more significantly, there is the impression that the gospel was slowly built up over a lengthy period and that, in its final form, it dates from the close of the first century.

Some recent scholars argue for a dependence of the fourth gospel on the synoptics, more plausibly on Mark. But it seems very difficult indeed to trace any direct relationship between John's gospel and the synoptic gospels. The Johannine tradition is, on the whole, independent. Even where it deals with matters also present in the synoptics, there is no obvious advertence to a synoptic parallel. The fourth evangelist has his own style of narration and formulation, and does not show any tendency to correct or replace the synoptics. Whether John had some knowledge of the traditional matter behind the synoptics is another question. We may surely assume the existence of cross-currents between the Johannine and synoptic traditions.

As regards the number of external facts recorded, the Johannine tradition is, in many respects, poorer than the synoptic. But it gives a notable amount of extra information which merits respect even from the historical point of view. The early stage or substratum of the Johannine tradition may be contemporaneous with the synoptic tradition. What we have in our present John is a later stage of development with a lengthy evolution of tradition behind it. John has a

9

special aim and this is the readiest explanation of his differences with the synoptists. Where he diverges from the synoptic accounts it is not only because he has a different and independent tradition at his disposal, but also because he is intent above all on his own theological purpose. Clement of Alexandria, in the early third century, characterised John as 'the spiritual gospel'. While one would question, seriously, his criterion, his designation may not be too wide of the mark. We adopt it in the context of this presentation.

The Beloved Disciple

At Jn 13:23 the Beloved Disciple (literally, 'the one whom Jesus loved') appears for the first time. Henceforth he will crop up regularly and always, explicitly or implicitly, in contrast to Peter. At the farewell meal he reclined next to Jesus and passed on Peter's question to Jesus (13:23-25). He may be that 'other disciple' who accompanied Peter and procured his entry into the court of the high priest (18:15-16). He stood, prominently, at the foot of the cross – Peter being conspicuously absent (19:25-27). The Beloved Disciple reached the tomb before Peter, and though the latter was first to enter the tomb it was the former alone 'who saw and believed' (20:2-10). Chapter 21 is built up around Peter and the Beloved Disciple. Though Peter has the more important role (vv 2, 3, 7, 11) it was the other who was sensitive in faith to the presence of the risen Jesus and recognised him (v 7). Peter asked of the Beloved Disciple: 'Lord, what about him?' (v 21). Evidently, behind the question lies the fact that the Disciple had died and a misunderstanding of a saying of Jesus is corrected (vv 22-23). At first sight, v 24 – 'This is the disciple who is testifying to these things and has written them' – would seem a formal claim to authorship. In fact, the Greek can quite well be understood in the sense that the Beloved Disciple is a witness to Jesus and source of the tradition behind the fourth gospel and the occasion of its writing. The evangelist was his disciple. Who this evangelist was, we do not know. We continue to name him conventionally: 'John'.

In summary: The fourth gospel had a complex genesis and grew in stages. Yet, it shows the signs of having been moulded by a dominant figure who shaped the traditional material to a particular theological cast and expression. We can be sure that for the Johannine community someone other than he, that is to say, the Beloved Disciple, a disciple of the ministry (not one of the Twelve) and source of the tradition, was the greatly revered link with Jesus. He stands, in contrast to Peter, as the father-figure of the Johannine group. The fourth gospel may have taken its final shape in Ephesus – where, also, the later epistles (1, 2, 3 John) would have been written. Its likely date: 90-100 AD.

Gospels

We have four gospels. In the past there had been a tendency to harmonise them, to smooth out discrepancies. This approach was largely motivated by the mistaken view that the gospels are biographical: the evangelists are telling the Jesus story 'as it actually happened'. In fact each gospel addresses the concerns and needs of specific communities. The readers know the basic story as well as the evangelist. He makes his point by telling the story in his way. It is story with plot and characters. Each of the evangelists tells essentially the same story, but the plots and emphases of the gospels differ widely. The events and actions of a story, its plot, often involve conflict, for conflict is at the heart of most stories. Not only do the gospels have plots, but the plot is, in a sense, the evangelist's interpretation of the story. As writers of narrative literature, the evangelists achieved their purpose by means of plot and characterisation. Jesus is always the chief character. The evangelist speaks, primarily, through him.

Tension

More recent study of the New Testament has brought to light not only evidence of rich pluralism. It has, more dramatically, unveiled evidence of tension and strife within Christian communities. There are sufficiently clear pointers to a turbulent history of the Johannine community. Fourth gospel and epistles witness to conflict: conflict of a Jewish-Christian group with fellow Jews and conflict within the Christian group. It is no petty squabbling. The evidence suggests that, for the most part, tension focused on the assessment of Jesus. Significantly, the question at issue had been raised in another gospel tradition: 'Who do you say that I am?' (Mk 8:29). Surely, for a Christian, this must ever be not only a question but an abiding

challenge. The question was faced and answered by the Johannine
community. Its answer was to have enormous repercussion on sub-
sequent Christianity, to our day. Indeed, it was later assumed that
Johannine Christians had given the christological answer. This
assumption needs to be looked at, carefully and critically.

Community

It emerges that the distinctive Johannine christology was hammered out in a process of making and defending claims for Jesus, a
Jesus who continued to loom more and more largely not only on the
community's horizon but at the heart of its life. If the fourth gospel
grew out of the lived faith of a Christian community – as indeed it
did – it must indeed help to look to the life of the community. 'Life'
is used advisedly as being sufficiently broad and vague. A term
such as 'history' would be misleading. It is surely not possible to
trace the history of a community that cannot be precisely identified
in the first place. Our only sources are the fourth gospel and the
epistles. We must read between the lines and what we read is a matter of discernment. What we discern may be close to the mark – or
wide of it. What encourages is that the findings of foremost
Johannine scholars approach something of a consensus. One
speaks, for convenience, of a Johannine community though not
thereby necessarily envisaging a single group. The movement
must, of course, have started as such, but certainly by the time of
the epistles (later than the gospel) and, surely too, through the
stages of the gospel, there would have been an association of
groups which may well have been geographically close.

'The Jews'

It is a truism that Christianity began as a movement within
Judaism. It ought come as no surprise to find in the fourth gospel
clear evidence of that origin. Throughout the gospel 'the Jews' figure largely; with a few exceptions the designation has a pejorative
ring. 'The Jews' are the implacable opponents of Jesus. Indeed,
Jesus himself seems no longer a Jew! At the same time the fourth
gospel is certainly not anti-Semitic – in the current sense. The evangelist and his Christians are themselves Jews. What we have is
something of a family quarrel. We may, with some confidence, dis-

cern its course. At first, a claim that Jesus was Messiah made by some Jews, while not accepted by other synagogue brothers and sisters, could be tolerated. The situation became tense when the Jesus followers began to make more and more daring claims on behalf of their Messiah.

The Jewish world of Jesus was pluralistic. Pharisees, Sadducees, Essenes, Baptist disciples are but some of the groups: Jews all of them, but with marked theological differences. At first Christians – Jewish Christians – would have fitted under the Jewish umbrella. The Jewish war of 66-70 AD changed all that. The destruction of Jerusalem and temple in 70 AD was a traumatic moment. Judaism had its back to the wall; there was no longer scope for tolerance. The pillars of Judaism were Torah (Law) and temple; now temple was gone. With the destruction of the temple the priesthood had lost its *raison d'être*. It may be assumed that while the Pharisees were mainly responsible for the survival of Judaism one can be reasonably sure that some of the temple priests had read the signs of the times and had made common cause with Pharisees who were building for the future. For their part the Pharisees, in the desperate situation after the Roman victory, would have welcomed support of former priests prepared to work with them. And this would seem to be the view of the fourth evangelist. In Jn 18:3, 12 'the chief priests and the Pharisees' are, surely, the same people as 'the Jews' named up to then. 'The Jews' are, in short, not contemporaries of Jesus but the leaders of a later Judaism vigorously opposed to the now distinctive Christian movement. This was during the closing decades of the first century and marks the climax of a fairly gradual development.

Conflict with Jews

The first Johannine Christians were, all of them, Jews who lived within the synagogue structure. They acknowledged Jesus as the fulfilment of Israel's hope and strenuously proclaimed their conviction. They maintained that Jesus was immeasurably superior to all of the religious figures of Israel – even Abraham and Moses. In debate with their fellow Jews they further pressed their claims for Jesus. He was the word of God (1:1) who alone had seen God (1:18; 6:46). Indeed, Jesus was 'making himself equal to God' (5:18; see

10:33). This is a Jewish misunderstanding of the Christian position because, in fact, John does not make Jesus equal to God as is clear from the section (5:19-30) immediately following the charge. For non-Christian Jews such claims were intolerable: one could not make such claims for Jesus and remain within the synagogue. The Johannine Christians found themselves expelled from the synagogue. In chapter 9 of John the parents of the man born blind will not be drawn into the quarrel 'because they were afraid of the Jews; for the Jews had already agreed that anyone who confessed Jesus to be the Messiah would be put out of the synagogue' (9:22; see 9:34). The same evidence emerges from 12:42; 16:2. One can no longer be a follower of Jesus and remain within this re-established Judaism.

Conflict within

A more bitter blow was when some within the community found the claim that Jesus was a descended heavenly being too much to take – they left (6:60-66). 'Many of his disciples exclaimed, "This is more than we can stand! How can anyone listen to such talk?" ... From that moment many of his disciples drew back and no longer went about with him.' Those who remained hardened their christological stance. For one thing, their emphasis on Jesus as one 'descended' from the heavenly world came to mean that he was 'not of this world' (see 17:16). Stress on the otherworldliness of Jesus meant that the significance of his life and death was obscured – a fact that surfaces in the Johannine epistles. These epistles tell of a further schism, again over the christological issue (see 1 Jn 2:18-19). And this is a very good reason why the fourth gospel should be taken in close association with the letters. It would seem, in fact, that the author of 1 John was largely responsible for having the fourth gospel eventually accepted by the church at large.

OUTLINE OF THE FOURTH GOSPEL

Prologue (1:1-18)
An introduction to the career of the incarnate Word.

The Book of Signs (1:19-12:50)
The public ministry of Jesus where in sign and word he shows himself to his own people as the revelation of his Father, only to be rejected.

A. The Opening Days of the Revelation of Jesus (1:19-51)
B. From Cana to Cana (2-4)
C. Jesus and the Feasts of 'the Jews' (5-10)
D. Jesus Moves Towards the Hour (11-12)

The Book of Glory (13-20)
To those who accept him Jesus shows his glory by returning to the
Father in 'the hour' of his crucifixion, resurrection and ascension.
Fully glorified, he communicates the Spirit of life.
A. Last Supper and Last Discourse (13-17)
B. The Passion (18-19)
C. The Resurrection (20:1-29)

Conclusion (20:30-31)

Epilogue (21)

THE MOVEMENT OF THOUGHT

The structure of the fourth gospel as a whole is notably dramatic.
This skillfulness of presentation is also present in the larger individ-
ual episodes, such as the Samaritan woman (4:1-42), the cure of the
blind man (ch 9), the raising of Lazarus (ch 11). In these episodes the
reader is brought stage by stage to a full revelation of Jesus. And the
reader, too, comes to an increasing certainty of faith. The longer
narrative complexes illustrate the conflicts of opinion, the antagonism between belief and unbelief. At the same time, these episodes
serve to present the great struggle between light and darkness, a
struggle in which, looked at from the outside, the powers of darkness and unbelief appear to be gaining the upper hand. Even in the
shorter passages such as the marriage at Cana (2:1-11), the cleansing
of the temple (2:13-22) and the healing of the official's son (4:46-54),
dramatic presentation is not lacking. Here, too, one finds the
moment of suspense before the liberating vision of faith.

An aspect of the dramatic in John is present in the emphasis placed
on 'signs'. The signs are mighty works performed in sight of Jesus'
disciples – miracles. Still, it is by contrasting 'miracle' and 'sign'
that we can best understand John's intention. The restoring of sight
to a blind man at Siloam (9:1-12) is indeed a miracle, quite like similar
miracles in the synoptics (see Mk 9:27-31). But John is not interested

in this or other miracles as such; his interest is in their symbolism, their signification. For him, the restoring of sight to a blind man is a sign of the spiritual light that Christ, who is Light, can give, because he viewed such actions of Jesus as pointers to a deeper, spiritual truth. We are not always left to work out these hidden meanings for ourselves because, in many cases, they are brought out in the discourses that accompany the signs. We are also thus provided with a criterion for judging other passages where such comment is lacking. The signs are clearly linked to the work of Jesus on earth; the purpose is to bring out the deeper dimensions of his works, to reveal the glory of the Son.

Nowhere does the difference between John and the synoptic gospels strike one more forcefully than in the discourses of Jesus. The discourses of the fourth gospel are quite distinctive. John does not reason in our western manner: he testifies, he affirms. He does not set out to prove a thesis by building up consecutive arguments until a conclusion is reached. Instead, his thought moves around a central point. John 14:1-24 can be taken as an example of how the thought 'circles', repeating and insisting, while, at the same time, moving forward and upward. Again, one may instance the 'parabolic discourses' – the Shepherd and the flock (10:1-18) and the Vine and the branches (15:1-10). Both passages are built on similar lines: first a presentation of the matter, the 'parable' (10:1-5; 15:1-2), followed by the typically Johannine development: a method of concentric thinking which flows in new circles. It is a meditative way of thought. It is a personal style evolved through meditation on the revelation of Jesus Christ.

Another notable feature of John is the frequent use of double or ambiguous expressions; this practice involves a clever technique. Such expressions, when spoken by Jesus, are first taken by his interlocutors in the obvious or natural sense and he proceeds to explain the deeper spiritual meaning. For example, in 2:19, the 'temple' of which Jesus speaks is not the building – as the Jews understood – but the temple of his body (2:21).

More characteristic, however, are such words as the adverb *anóthen* (3:3, 7) which means 'again' (and was so understood by Nicodemus, and also 'from above' the meaning really intended by Jesus). The rendering of the adverb qualifies the meaning of 'birth' (3:3, 7) and this is also misunderstood by Nicodemus. In 3:14 we read of the Son of Man being 'lifted up'. The same expression occurs in 8:28 and 12:32-33; in the latter case a note makes clear that crucifixion is meant. The evangelist regards the 'elevation' of Jesus on the cross as a symbol of his 'elevation' to heaven by his resurrection and ascension. In John's eyes, the death, resurrection and exaltation of Christ are aspects of one and the same mystery. Hence, he can regard the exaltation on the cross and the exaltation in glory as one movement.

In interpreting the fourth gospel we must be careful to give full weight to this technique of the evangelist. We should realise that he has chosen these expressions precisely because they have more than one signification and that he really intends the two (or more) meanings of each expression. We should not be true to his mind if we were to narrow his meaning to one or other alternative. If John uses ambiguous words it is not because he wants to be obscure or wishes to hide something. Quite the opposite is true because what he does is to look beyond the superficial sense of an expression to a deeper, spiritual meaning. This method is to be understood in much the same manner as his presentation of signs; not only the actions of Jesus, but his words too are 'signs'. It is because they are words of Christ – 'words of eternal life' (6:68) – that they have a deeper meaning, and this truth can be effectively symbolised by the use of double expressions.

JOHANNINE THEOLOGY

John has indicated, firmly, the purpose of his gospel: 'These [signs] are written so that you may continue to believe that Jesus is the Messiah, the Son of God, and that through believing you may have life in his name' (20:31). Obviously, he has sought to stress faith in the person of Jesus Christ and in his salvific power. The foundation of that faith is his own presentation of the facts, his choice among many other signs which Jesus had wrought (20:30). His intent is to bring people to believe, more profoundly, that this man of flesh and blood, Jesus of Nazareth, is the Messiah of Jewish expectation – and something far, far more than that. 'That you may continue to believe' looks to those who already believed – who have believed without seeing (20:29) – inviting them to a more profound and stable faith. This faith is directed to the living and glorified Lord, preached by the church, living in the church. He is the Saviour, the Lord of glory – and none other than the Jesus of the gospel. Faith in him has power to bestow salvation, life 'in his name'.

The Johannine world is characterised by division into light and darkness, life and death. It is clear that John's dualism has nothing to do with philosophical speculation on good and evil but is a component of salvation history. This warfare between light and darkness is not cosmic but is a struggle within humans in a search for truth and life. In the Johannine view, truth has come, whole and entire, with the coming of the Son. In him the meeting of God with humankind has taken place: he is the communication of divine life. The truth, light and life which humankind need have been brought by the Son; they are given because he is one with humankind.

For John the story of Jesus is that place in history where the ultimate truth about God is to be found. More than the synoptists it is he who gives us an awareness of this through his theme of life. John had more to tell about Jesus than any gospel could hold. He had glimpsed the divine light which, all the while, irradiated the Teacher from Nazareth.

The incarnation is a beginning. It has to be fulfilled in the work for which the Son had been sent into the world: the glorification – revelation – of the Father that in turn is the glorification/revelation of the Son. The 'hour' of Jesus, the hour of his suffering and death, is one phase of his 'glorification', the other being his resurrection and going to the Father. Now he is revealed for who he really is. In contrast to the synoptists, John has underlined the 'glorification' aspect of the passion story. It is an hour of triumph because, despite appearances, it is the 'world' – unbelieving humankind – that stands judged and the power of evil broken. The incarnate Word has revealed God by his words and deeds – and has himself been revealed.

Faith

Faith has a supremely important place in John's theology. Faith, of course, is equally emphasised by Paul, but the accent is different. For one thing, John prefers the verb 'to believe', while Paul favours the noun 'faith'. Perhaps John wants to stress that faith is less an internal disposition than an active commitment; but surely Paul would concur. More significant is the fact that, for Paul, faith in the crucified and risen Lord is all-important. John projects this faith on to his account of the earthly work of Jesus and shows it unfolding in personal encounter with the redeemer during his earthly life. He is careful, though, to bring out its bearing on the time after Easter as he does in Jesus' concluding statement: 'Blessed are those who have not seen and yet believe' (20:29). Still, by his projecting Christian faith into the time of Jesus' ministry, John can strikingly and effectively describe exactly the beginning and the growth of faith, the motives that inspire it, the dangers that threaten it. He can show that Jesus himself demands faith as the one thing necessary for salvation and can make it clear that faith is faith in Jesus as the one in whom God has revealed himself. And he also brings out that faith is rooted in this historical and incarnational revelation. It is precisely because of this incarnational dimension that Paul and John are one in asserting that faith must become effective in love. 'For in Christ Jesus neither circumcision nor uncircumcision counts for anything; the only thing that counts is faith working through love' (Gal 5:6). And, in John, brotherly/sisterly charity becomes the 'new commandment' of Jesus (Jn 13:34-35).

The most distinctive and the most frequent Johannine faith expression is *pisteuein eis,* 'to believe in.' The usage brings out the most marked characteristic of Johannine faith – faith is directed exclusively to the person of Jesus. To believe means to receive and accept Jesus' self-revelation; it means to attach oneself to him, in personal union, in order to receive from him eternal life; it means total commitment to him. It is so much more than trust or confidence in him. The believer can have the fullest assurance as one finds, in the very object of one's faith, the deepest motive for and the surest foundation of faith. For this Son is attested by the Father, attests himself in response to the Father, and is continually attested in the apostolic testimony.

The personal union of the believer with Christ is also expressed by other terms which can stand for Johannine faith. It emerges clearly in the parallelism of 6:35 that 'to believe' in Jesus is to come to him: 'I am the bread of life. Whoever comes to me will never be hungry, and whoever believes in me will never be thirsty.' Faith can also be described as 'hearing' the voice or the words of Jesus – hearing and obeying. The believer abides in the word – and in Jesus himself (8:31). Believing is also seeing. More than any other New Testament writer, John has laid stress on faith as vision; it is a true vision of God, of Truth. Faith and knowledge are often associated, but they are not identical. 'Faith', whose object is a Person, can certainly grow into 'knowledge' for, in biblical thought, 'to know' is always an act which institutes or reinforces fellowship. Knowledge comes through faith, and faith should grow into knowledge – more intimate relationship with Father and Son. And because the revelation of God in Christ is pre-eminently the revelation of his love, there is the closest possible connection between faith and love.

CHAPTER 2

The Johannine Jesus

The word became flesh and lived among us (Jn 1:14)

The fourth gospel was a major factor in the elaboration of trinitarian theology and christology at the councils of Ephesus (431) and Chalcedon (451). These councils were centuries later than our gospel. Our concern is the Jesus of John. His understanding of Jesus was quite independent of these later developments. The fourth gospel cannot be the starting-point of christology for the very good reason that it is not. The scholarly view is that John is the latest of our gospels. Christology had begun even before Mark, our earliest gospel. It had started with Paul.

It is clear that John is narrating the story of a post-resurrection Jesus. The Jesus of the fourth gospel is, in effect, the risen Lord retrojected into the time of Jesus' earthly ministry. The one the evangelist has in mind is the risen, exalted Lord who, here and now, exists in the mode of God, that of Spirit. The origin of John's christology is that Christian Easter experience of the risen Christ. The claims of the Johannine Jesus are the claims of the Christ of faith. In the fourth gospel God (*ho theos*) is the Father; the Son is the one whom he has sent, his revealer. In Jesus, God has become visible; God has become historically transparent in this 'Son'. Jesus, in his earthly life, is revelation of the invisible Father. What John is doing is to say, simultaneously, that Jesus is fully human and is also fully the revelation of God.

In John the divinity of Jesus is always in the background. Throughout the gospel Jesus displays omniscience, refers to his pre-existent life and speaks and behaves like the risen Lord. The term 'pre-existence' is unfortunate. It leads to the misunderstanding that

the person of Jesus Christ can be split into 'eternal Son' and 'temporal Son.' What is eternal, 'pre-existent', is the Word of God, not the
person of Jesus of Nazareth – the Word being God's eternal commitment to be personally present in history. God wills to share his
own life and his very self. The divinity of Jesus is not some kind of
second substance in him. He is the human person who is the manifestation and presence of God in our world.

The declaration, 'I and the Father are one' (10:30) is not intended to
be a metaphysical statement on the unity of Father and Son. Rather,
John's concern is a unity of revelation between Father and Son. As
the one sent and as revealer, Jesus is the eternal Word of God, eternal Son of God. Jesus of Nazareth is the Logos of God in person, and
he is Logos in his humanness. Now, to how the distinctive
Johannine christology was hammered out.

JOHANNINE CHRISTOLOGY

We have observed that there was conflict within the Johannine
community, mainly concerning its understanding of Jesus. We are
warned that Johannine christology needs to be carefully and critically
assessed. It was problematic from the start.

Contrast

Comparison with the other gospels – indeed with the rest of the
New Testament – is of first importance. While one acknowledges
that the portrait of Jesus in the synoptic gospels is already, and
inevitably, coloured by Easter faith, the Jesus of John is startlingly
different. Contrast is sharpest between Mark and John. One need
but compare the two passion narratives, beginning with the arrest
of Jesus (Mk 14:43-50; Jn 18-19) to see that the stories are historically
incompatible. A look at the brief accounts of the arrest will suffice to
make the point.

> Immediately, while he was still speaking, Judas, one of the
> twelve, arrived; and with him there was a crowd with swords
> and clubs, from the chief priests, the scribes and the elders. Now
> the betrayer had given them a sign, saying, 'The one I will kiss is
> the man; arrest him and lead him away under guard.' So when
> he came, he went up to him and said, 'Rabbi!' and kissed him.

Then they laid hands on him and arrested him. But one of those who stood near drew his sword and struck the slave of the high priest, cutting off his ear. Then Jesus said to them, 'Have you come out with swords and clubs to arrest me as though I were a bandit? Day after day I was with you in the temple teaching, and you did not arrest me. But let the scriptures be fulfilled.' All of them deserted him and fled (Mk 14:43-50).

The story-line: Jesus is 'still speaking' his closing words of the Gethsemane episode (14:32-42). Judas plays an essential role, leading the arresting crowd to where Jesus was to be found and then, at nightime and in a group, identifying the right man. Jesus, quite passive, was at once arrested. The unnamed slave of the high priest was wounded by one of the bystanders; Mark gives the impression of a clumsy stroke by someone other than a disciple. Jesus, now a prisoner, does protest at the timing and manner of his arrest: he is not a man of violence and there was no call for this show of force. All the frightened disciples deserted him.

After Jesus had spoken these words, he went out with his disciples across the Kidron valley to a place where there was a garden, which he and his disciples entered. Now Judas, who betrayed him, also knew the place, because Jesus often met there with his disciples. So Judas brought a detachment of soldiers together with police from the chief priests and the Pharisees, and they came there with lanterns and torches and weapons. Then Jesus, knowing all that was to happen to him, came forward and asked them, 'Whom are you looking for?' They answered, 'Jesus of Nazareth.' Jesus replied, 'I am.' Judas, who betrayed him, was standing with them. When Jesus said to them, 'I am,' they stepped back and fell to the ground. Again he asked them, 'Whom are you looking for?' And they said, 'Jesus of Nazareth.' Jesus answered, 'I told you that I am.' So if you are looking for me, let these men go. This was to fulfil the word he had spoken, 'I did not lose a single one of those whom you gave me.' Then Simon Peter, who had a sword, drew it, struck the high priest's slave, and cut off his right ear. The slave's name was Malchus. Jesus said to Peter, 'Put your sword back into its sheath. Am I not to drink the cup that the Father has given me?' (Jn 18:1-11).

The story-line: Here reference to the 'words' of Jesus points not to
Gethsemane (an episode absent from the fourth gospel) but to the
solemn prayer of John 17. Judas guides not a 'crowd' but a (Roman)
military detachment, as well as temple police. Jesus, fully aware of
all that was to happen, takes the initiative and strides forward to
accost the band of soldiers and police; there is no need for Judas to
identify him, as is expressly noted. They are seeking 'Jesus of
Nazareth.' At the God-presence in him, manifest in his declaration
'I am', they are rendered powerless – stricken to the ground. Jesus,
completely in command of the situation, lays down his terms: they
may arrest him, on condition that they do not detain the disciples.
These do not desert him, as in Mark; he protects them. It is 'Simon
Peter' who strikes out and cuts off the right ear of 'Malchus' – the
story has grown from its Marcan form. Jesus rebukes Peter (instead
of protesting at the manner of his own arrest, as in Mark). Only now
is Jesus arrested, and only because he permitted it to happen.

CHRISTOLOGIES

It is evidently the same incident, but how different the telling. The
fact is: each version is comfortably at home in its proper setting; it
just would not do to switch the accounts. This alerts one to the manner of proper understanding. There is little doubt that Mark's version is closer to what really happened. It would, however, be a mis-
take to imagine that Mark is primarily concerned with 'facts' and
that, consequently, he does not propose a christology; or that, at
best, he puts forward a 'low' christology. It is one of the unfortunate
results of such a concentration on the Johannine picture that the
christology of the other evangelists has been under-rated. Indeed,
the Marcan christology is not 'inferior' to the Johannine. It is
notably different.[3]

Fleeting reference above to Gethsemane suggests a further point of
comparison. In Mk 14:32-36 we encounter a shattered Jesus, crushed
to the point of death at the prospect of a gruesome fate. He prayed,
explicitly, that 'this hour might pass him by'. He needed to be
assured that the path which opened before him was indeed the way
that God would have him walk. John, on the other hand, though
clearly aware of the Gethsemane tradition, studiously avoids the
Gethsemane episode. He has Jesus declare: 'Now my soul is trou-

bled. And what should I say – "Father, save me from this hour?"' (Jn 12:27). So far, reminiscent of Mark. Then comes a distinctively Johannine twist: 'No, it was for this reason that I have come to this hour.' The Johannine Jesus refused to pray the Gethsemane prayer. It is inconceivable that he could speak the words of Mk 14:36 because the Johannine Jesus 'knows all that was to happen to him' (Jn 18:4). Again, there is a clash of christologies. For us, it is not a matter of choosing between them. It is, rather, a question of under-standing both of them. Here our concern is the Johannine Jesus.

THE JOHANNINE JESUS

The distinctiveness of the Johannine Jesus is evident from the first line of the fourth gospel. He is the incarnate Logos – the human presence of God in the world. Jesus is the new temple: meeting-place of God and humankind – the 'place' of true worship (see 2:13-22; 4:20-24). He has replaced the feasts of Israel; he is the light of the world (chs 7-9). He is the Good Shepherd who lays down his life for his sheep (ch 10). He is the way to the Father, the true way, the way of life (ch 14). As genuine vine he is life-source of his disciples (ch 15). He is the one, lifted up from the earth, who draws all to himself (8:28; 12:32). He pours out the life-giving Spirit (7:37-39; 19:34-35).

As one come down from heaven Jesus, from the start, seems an otherworldly figure. Admittedly, he can be found sitting wearily by a well (4:6). He is a man who 'loved Martha and her sister and Lazarus' (11:5). But these are rare flashes. It is the majestic Word-made-flesh who moves through the pages of John. The passion nar-rative (chs 18-19) effectively illustrates the distinctiveness of this Jesus. John presents the passion as the triumph of the Son of God. Jesus is firmly in control. He is the Judge who judges his judge (Pilate) and his accusers ('the Jews'). He is the King who reigns, with the cross for a throne.

In general, John and the synoptics tell the same story, but tell it differ-ently. While already in Matthew and Luke there is a tendency to stress what one might call the otherworldliness of Jesus, in John he seems something of a sojourner from another world. In the synoptic gospels Jesus' message concerns the 'kingdom of God,' the benevo-lent rule of God. In John, what Jesus preaches, what he reveals, is himself. Jesus is still concerned to make the real God known, but now what God is can be found and seen in Jesus himself. True, it is in and through Jesus we come to know God, but the Johannine emphasis is unique: 'No one has ever seen God; God's only Son, who is nearest to the Father's heart, has made him known' (1:18). There is a series of 'I am' sayings (e.g. 'I am the bread of life,' 6:35; see 10:11; 11:25 ...). This reaches its height in the four absolute 'I am' sayings (8:24, 28, 58; 13:19) – e.g. 'When you have lifted up the Son of Man, then you will realise that I AM' (8:28). Each time there is an echo of the divine name of Ex 3:14 or, more immediately, of Is 43:10-11. Jesus declares: I am the bearer of God's name and power. We must not lose sight of the fact that, throughout the fourth gospel, Jesus' subordination to the Father is just as clearly expressed (e.g. 5:19, 26).

The One Sent

For John, Jesus is the 'one sent'. He is agent of the Father, empowered to speak and act in the name of the Father. This role of agent explains otherwise contradictory statements in the fourth gospel. Tension is sharpest in the contrast of two terse declarations: 'The Father and I are one' (10:30); 'The Father is greater than I' (14:28). When we read them in the light of the role of agent and against other texts throughout the gospel, we appreciate that there is no contradiction.

The Johannine Jesus is always conscious of being the 'one sent'. His statements are unambiguous: 'I seek to do not my own will, but the will of him who sent me' (5:30). If he freely lays down his life it is because 'I have received this command from my Father' (10:18). He is Son, apprenticed to his Father; he has learned everything from his Father: 'The Son can do nothing on his own, but only what he sees the Father doing; for whatever the Father does, the Son does likewise' (5:19). 'The Father loves the Son and shows him all that he himself is doing' (5:20). It is precisely because he is agent, plenipotent representative of the Father, that he is the living presence of that Father; he has received the Father's name and power. 'Know and understand that the Father is in me and I in the Father' (12:38); 'Whoever has seen me has seen the Father' (14:9). He is God's son because he is the one 'whom the Father has sanctified and sent into the world' (10:36). Jesus speaks the I AM as the one who bears God's name and wields his power. In him God, the everlasting one, is revealed and made present.

Revealer of the Father, Jesus is not identical with the Father. Here is where the statement, 'The Father is greater than I' (14:28) fits in. The priority of the Father comes from the fact that Jesus' power comes from him. But what is one to make of the confession, 'My Lord and my God' (20:28) at the close of the gospel? Thomas was reacting, in wonder and praise, to the God who was so dramatically revealed in the risen Jesus.

The Logos

There still remains the Word. A traditional starting-point of christ-ology is the Johannine statement *ho logos sarx egeneto* – the Word became flesh, became a human person (Jn 1:14). The Logos, the Word, was with God from the beginning and was God's agent in creation. The background here is Old Testament Wisdom; the fig-ure of Wisdom is the most developed personification in Jewish tradition. Wisdom is a personification of God's own self – God's active and gracious presence in the world. In John the Logos assumes the role which had been attributed to Wisdom. Logos is God's eternal commitment to be personally present in history. Jesus of Nazareth is the concrete shape and form which God's eternal intent has taken.

As the one who makes God uniquely present, as Revealer of God, Jesus is God's only Son. Perhaps the prologue of Hebrews puts the matter better. In the past God spoke at various times and in many ways through the prophets. In the fullness of time he has spoken in the person of his Son – who is 'the reflection of God's glory and the exact imprint of God's very being' (Heb 1:3). Jesus is the manifesta-tion and presence of God in our world. This is why the whole reality of Jesus may not be adequately summed up under the designation 'human being' – there is something other, something much more. But his human wholeness must be acknowledged. In the fourth gospel this dimension is blurred.

THE JOHANNINE ICON

The synoptists wrote out of their Easter faith but they, to an extent, have allowed the historical Jesus to be seen and to speak. John, for his part, has imposed wholly the Christ of faith upon the earthly

Jesus. He has painted an icon. An icon does not aim at literal representation; it is consciously stylised. An icon brings out the spiritual significance of the subject. The Johannine Icon, then, represents the Jesus of faith, the risen Lord. As well, the fourth evangelist has put into the mouth of his Jesus the theological significance of what the earthly Jesus had meant. His Jesus is an icon of the Christ of faith; the words of his Jesus are words of the risen Lord. In short, the Johannine Jesus is wholly the Christ of our post-resurrection faith experience.

A. T. Hanson offers an intriguing assessment of the Johannine christology:

> What John has done is to depict a Jesus who is the mouthpiece for John's christology, but he does cast his work in the form of a gospel, with prologue, miracles, teaching, passion, death and resurrection. Consequently, the fourth gospel is from one point of view the gospel for the weaker believers, not for the stronger. Far from being a secret teaching, it is a teaching suitable for those who cannot take the scandal of the full humanity of Jesus. Tougher (and deeper) minds can stand the *kenosis* of Paul, and the grim realism of Mark. Weaker minds cannot, and as the majority of Christians in any age will belong to the weaker group, John's gospel has become the dominant one. The church's traditional picture of Jesus down the ages has been John's picture weakly qualified by the Jesus of the synoptics.[4]

CHAPTER 3

The Beginning

Do whatever he tells you (Jn 2:5)

THE PROLOGUE (1:1-18)

The prologue of the fourth gospel, a hymn, tells us that Jesus Christ is the incarnation of the Word and introduces the basic themes (life, light, darkness, truth, witness, glory, the world) which will be developed throughout the gospel. Since it only affirms, it cannot be fully understood until the gospel as a whole has been read.

The first part of the passage (vv 1-11) presents the Son as the Word who brings life from God and as the light who reveals God. The Word was eternally present with God, the creative Wisdom of God (vv 3-5, 9). The Baptist is a voice that sounds, summoning 'all' to faith in that Word present in Jesus (vv 6-8). The unbelieving world and the Jewish people turned from the light (vv 9-11) – a negative response that will recur throughout the gospel.

The second part (vv 12-18) notes the positive response leading to a sharing in life, a sharing that will make believers to be children of God. This has come about because the heavenly Word took on our human existence and 'pitched his tent' among us. Those who have received him have seen his 'glory': his filial love for his Father and the divine life which he possesses as Son, and the revelation of that love and life. Those who believe in him receive lavishly of his full-ness. They have the gift of truth ('grace and truth'): the revelation of divine life and love as it is a living reality in the Son. And all because the Son alone can make the Father known – for he alone is 'the reflection of God's glory and the exact imprint of God's very being' (Heb 1:3).

The prologue depicts Jesus primarily as the one who manifests the

Father to men and women. Since he alone was with God (v 1) and since he alone has seen God (v 18), he alone could reveal the full truth about God. Unlike the synoptists who presented Jesus as the Messiah who inaugurates the kingdom of God, John will continue in the rest of the gospel to present Jesus primarily as the Revealer of the Father and of the Father's plan of salvation.

'In the beginning was the word': the opening words of John's gospel recall Genesis 1:1. In the Old Testament God's word manifested him: in creation, in deeds of power, in prophecy. Perhaps even more evocatively, behind John's Logos ('word') and the Prologue as a whole, is the striking personification of Wisdom, notably in Job 28; Proverbs 8; Sirach 24; Baruch 3:9-4:4; Wisdom 7:22-8:1.

The Lord begot Wisdom as the first-born:

> The Lord begot me as the beginning of his work,
> the first of his acts of long ago. (Prov 8:22)

> I came forth from the mouth of the Most High. (Sir 24:3)

Wisdom was intimately associated with the work of creation:

> When he established the heavens, I was there ...
> I was beside him like a master worker ...
> rejoicing in his inhabited world
> and delighting in the human race. (Prov 8:27, 30-31)

The privileged abode of Wisdom is Israel:

> I took root in an honoured people,
> in the portion of the Lord, his heritage. (Sir 24:12)

The intimate relationship of Wisdom with God is expressed in a remarkable manner in Wis 7:25-26:

> She is a breath of the power of God,
> and a pure emanation of the glory of the Almighty ...
> She is a reflection of eternal light,
> a spotless mirror of the working of God,
> and an image of his goodness.

Much of this echoes in the Prologue. What is most significant is that Wisdom is best understood as a communication of God. And Logos, 'word', is essentially about communication.

John shows that Jesus Christ, the incarnate Word, is the ultimate revelation of God. The term Logos is a signal that a word of revelation will be spoken. The Word was 'turned toward God' (Jn 1:1) – was in relationship with God; yet, Word and God are distinct. The Word makes God known in creation and in the human story. The Word gives true life; a life that is authentic light, illuminating and giving direction to the human way. The Word came into the world, came among his own people only to be ignored and rejected (vv 10-11). Some, however, received the Word by believing in Jesus. These were granted to be children of God – here and now. These can see the revelation of God in his Son, Jesus Christ.

'And the Word became flesh and lived among us' (v 14): the Word entered our history. 'He lived among us' is, literally, 'he pitched his tent among us'; John recalls Yahweh's dwelling among the Israelites in the Tent of Meeting (Ex 33:7-11). 'Glory' (*kabod*) is another expression of God's presence (see Ex 40:34; 1 Kg 8:11) – the manifestation of Yahweh to his people. 'We have seen his glory' (Jn 1:14): John uses *doxa*, the Greek rendering of the Hebrew word. To gaze on the incarnate Word was to see the revelation of the divine in the human story.

The 'glory' of the Word is the full revelation of the divine. While the torah of Moses was revelation and gift (*charis*), it has been replaced by a greater gift – 'a gift in place of a gift' (v 16). The fullness of gift, the definitive revelation of God, has taken place in Jesus Christ. Though Israel might claim that great ones like Abraham and Moses had seen God, it is the only Son who has truly known him (v 18). 'There is only one historical figure who has told the story of God's way with the world: the only begotten Son. Throughout the story that is about to be told the Son's attention will be unbrokenly focused on the Father.'[5]

THE FIRST DAYS OF JESUS' MINISTRY (1:19-51)

The Book of Signs opens with the beginning of Jesus' ministry. The passage falls into a pattern of four days: 1:19-28, 29-34, 35-42, 43-51. The phrase, 'the next day' in v 29 indicates that the questioning of the Baptist happened on day one. The first part of the passage (vv 19-28) is the Baptist's vehement negative testimony: he is not the Messiah! Nor is he Elijah – traditionally, on the basis of Mal 3:1; 4:5, expected to precede the Messiah. And he is not the prophet-like-Moses, another messianic precursor (see Deut 18:15,18). He is a voice, only a heraldic voice – and yet the solemn voice of the wilderness prophet of Isaiah 63. If he baptises it is with water: an acknowledgment that one has repented. He is no more than a slave whose task it is to untie his master's sandal; and he feels unworthy even of that. There is polemic here. Not John himself but disciples of the Baptist who still claimed John as Messiah are being put in their place (see Acts 19:1-4).

On day two (vv 29-34) the Baptist bore witness to Jesus as the Lamb of God and Son of God. He is 'the Lamb of God who takes away the sin of the world' (v 29). The operative phrase is 'of God'; in biblical thought only God takes away or forgives sin (see Mk 2:7). By 'lamb of God' the Baptist has in mind the Passover lamb (Jn 19:14). He may, too, have in mind the Servant of the Lord who is compared to a lamb in Is 53:7-12. For that matter, within the broader sacrificial system, a lamb figured regularly in rites of reconciliation and communion after sin. More than likely, the evangelist had all of this rich background in mind. In any event, Jesus is the one who will destroy the sin that envelops humankind, but he does so as Lamb of God. He is the Son of God on whom the Spirit descended and rested – he has permanent possession of the Spirit (see Is 11:2; 42:1). He will 'baptise' by sharing his spirit. The evangelist knows that the glorified Jesus bestowed the Spirit (Jn 20:22)

On the third day (vv 35-42) two disciples of the Baptist 'followed' Jesus; in the gospels *akolouthein*, 'to follow', means discipleship. Andrew and Simon were now Jesus' disciples. This has implications for the view that Jesus himself had been a disciple of the Baptist.[6] Two titles emerge: Rabbi (v 37) and Messiah (v 41). These are inadequate titles. Even 'Messiah' does not measure up to the status of the Jesus of the Prologue, nor to the Baptist's Lamb of God and Son of God. 'What are you looking for?' Jesus asks, and bids the seekers 'come and see' (v 38). To 'come to' Jesus (see 3:18-21) and to 'see' him (see 14:9) is the active movement towards the person of the Lord, and the understanding in faith of who he is. Though the first to answer the call was Andrew, attention focuses on the initiative of Jesus who designated (by a significant change of name) Peter for a future supportive role in the Christian community.

On the fourth day (vv 43-51) 'Jesus decided to go to Galilee'; the initiative passes from the Baptist to him. He called a disciple – Philip. For Philip, Jesus is 'he about whom Moses in the law and even the prophets wrote' (v 45) – a manifestly traditional understanding of messiahship. Nor is Nathanael's 'Rabbi, you are the Son of God! You are the King of Israel' (v 49) any more than an expression of Jewish messianic hope. All the titles in vv 38-49 fall short of the true Johannine assessment. In Gen 28:12-17 Jacob dreamt of a stairway linking heaven and earth; ascending and descending 'angels' symbolised the contact between God and his earthly creation. The place of the vision was Bethel ('house of God') – the 'gate of heaven.' Here in v 51 the Son of Man – Jesus' self-designation – is now the gate of heaven, the communication between God and humankind. This is who he truly is.[7]

FROM CANA TO CANA (2:1-4:54)

The title of this section is apposite because the second Cana miracle (4:43-54) is firmly linked with the story of Jesus' first visit to Cana: 'Now this was the second sign that Jesus did after coming from Judea to Galilee' (v 54).

First Miracle of Cana (2:1-12)

The first character in the story, the mother of Jesus, initiated the action with her implied request: 'They have no wine.' Jesus' response was abrupt: 'Woman, what concern is that to you and to me?' It draws a sharp line between Jesus and his mother. The second part of his response underlines this and suggests the reason: 'My hour has not yet come.' The 'hour' of Jesus, which unfolds throughout the gospel, is at the pleasure of the Father. The mother stands outside the world of Father and Son. All the more surprising, then, is the mother's reaction: 'His mother said to the servants, "Do whatever he tells you".' Wholly unaware of her son's role in God's design, she nevertheless demands that anything he asks should be done. 'She is the first person in the narrative to show, at the level of the action of the story, that the correct response to the person of Jesus is trust in his word ... She trusts unconditionally, indeed even in face of apparent rejection and rebuke, in the efficacy of the word of Jesus.'[8]

The water 'for the Jewish rites of purification' turned into wine, symbolises the old order which yields place to the new. For the evangelist the narrative is the symbol of something that occurs throughout the whole of Jesus' ministry – the manifestation of the 'glory' of Jesus. Revelation in John is the self-revelation of Jesus (ultimately, revelation of the Father); all the rest stems from this. The significance of the wine is that it is Jesus' gift, a sign which comes from him and points to him. As a gift of Jesus the wine is, significantly, given at the end; so precious and copious, it is the eschatological gift of the Messiah. The evangelist is not referring to any particular gift (such as the eucharist) but to Jesus himself as Revealer. If at this, 'the first of his signs', Jesus 'manifested his glory and his disciples believed in him' this was but a beginning. The full manifestation will not be until 'the hour'. The disciples have much, very much to learn.

Cleansing the Temple (2:13-21)

The cleansing of the temple which John has set at an early stage of Jesus' ministry is, more credibly, put by the synoptists at the close of the ministry (Mk 11:15-18 and parr.). What matters is not when it happened but what it means. Jesus passed judgment on the Jewish sacrificial system. By word and deed, in the fashion of Old Testament prophets (Jer 7:11; Mal 3:1), he protests against the profanation of God's house and signals that its messianic purification is at hand. 'The Jews' – the hostile religious authorities – recognise that Jesus' action was the deed of one who was a prophet and claimed to be Messiah.

John spelled out the significance of the deed. He recalled the words of Ps 69:10: 'Zeal for your house will consume me.' The symbolic action had been predicted for the messianic age by Zech 14:21: 'there should no longer be traders in the house of the Lord of hosts on that day.' After the resurrection (Jn 2:17, 22) the full meaning of what Jesus did and said became clear to his followers. Jesus, the risen Messiah, had taken the place of the temple and all it stood for. The centre of God's presence among his people is no longer a place; it is henceforth a person (see 4:21-24). The new sanctuary is the risen body of Jesus. In this new temple dwells the fullness of the Spirit. And that Spirit comes to those who believe and dwells with them so that they, in their turn, become temples of God.

Jesus and Nicodemus (3:1-21)

The dialogue with Nicodemus treats of new birth. Nicodemus, 'a Pharisee' and 'a ruler of the Jews' came to Jesus 'by night'. He came out of darkness towards the light. He was well disposed but was blinkered by his theology (v 9). This is the first step in Nicodemus' journey to faith (see 7:50-52; 19:39-42). Jesus played on the double meaning of *anóthen*: 'again', 'from above'; typically, John intends both meanings. True to the procedure of the gospel, Nicodemus understood the statement of Jesus at its surface level (v 4); Jesus then explained that he meant spiritual rebirth from above. His baptism, which brings about this rebirth is not in water only – as was the baptism of John – but of 'water and the Spirit' (v 5). The Christian reader would appreciate the need of both ritual water baptism and spiritual experience of 'the Spirit'. Then comes an enigmatic reference to the death of Jesus (vv 14-15) and a clear statement of the marvellous love of God (vv 16-18).

In v 14 John gives a double significance to the verb 'to be lifted up'. Firstly, it means the physical fact of being raised up on the cross, just as the bronze figure of a serpent was raised by Moses over the stricken Israelites (Num 21:4-9). But it also evokes the spiritual elevation of Jesus by the Father. Paradoxically, Jesus' death will also be his elevation and his 'glorification': the supreme moment of revelation. Like the bronze serpent of old, the Son of Man will be the effective sign of salvation for all who look on him with trust.

Verses 16-21 develop what had gone before. The hope of salvation offered through the descent and exaltation of the Son of Man is now traced back to its ultimate source: God's marvellous love. It was God who set the process in motion, wishing that the world might be rescued from sin. Verse 16 ('God so loved the world ...') is the very foundation of the gospel. Together with 1 :14 ('the Word was made flesh') and 12:32 ('I, when I am lifted up from the earth, will draw all people to myself'), it constitutes the 'good news' proclaimed by John.

God's love reaches out to all of humankind – that is its range. The expression of his love in the uniquely precious gift of his Son is the measure of its depth. The Father had given his only Son to the world out of love. It is the Father, therefore, who initiates the work of human redemption. John underlines the fact that Jesus is the object of all the love of the Father when he refers to Jesus as the 'only' Son. Verse 17 develops this idea. God's love is shown by sending his Son on a mission of salvation. He had not been sent to judge, that is, to condemn: he had come to save. A condition must be fulfilled on the human side – we must believe in Jesus as the only Son of God, Revealer of the Father. We must accept Jesus totally for who and what he is. Faith is a movement towards Jesus, a movement that leaves one open to the 'life' that comes uniquely from him.

Yet, not everyone will benefit from the loving initiative of God; some, by hardening their hearts against belief in Jesus, will seal their own condemnation (vv 18-21). Jesus brings judgment with him, necessarily; he is like a light that shines into the heart of each person, and the way we react to this light determines our destiny. If, loving darkness and deceit and selfish ways, we turn wilfully from God's light, we cannot come to God; we renounce the right to be called his children. For John, salvation or damnation begin already here on earth, according to one's acceptance or rejection of Jesus, the only Son of God. The essential judgment is not passed by Jesus (or by the Father) but is implied in the choice we make when we are confronted by him. Is it really as cut and dried as this?

Rather like Deuteronomy with its doctrine of the Two Ways (Deut 30:15-20) – 'See, I have set before you today life and death ... If you obey the commandments of the Lord your God ... then you shall live ... but if your heart turns away ... you shall perish ... I call heaven and earth to witness against you today that I have set before you life and death' – the fourth gospel is very much white and black. The choice is stark. In John we must come to the Light, or turn away; there is no grey area. In each case, Deuteronomy and John, the statement is powerful. Happily, the synoptists and Paul (and the biblical writers in general) are more alert to the fact that life is much more complex. More often than not our response in discipleship embraces failure. I find support in the vulnerable Jesus of Mark. The Jesus of Luke is, notoriously, friend of sinners (see Lk 15). There is our comfort. With their help, I can live with John's Jesus.

Jesus and the Baptist (3:22-36)

The verses 22-36 provide information about Jesus not found else-where in the gospel tradition. He moved into the Judean country-side and engaged in a ministry of baptism while, at the same time, John the Baptist was active in Samaria. Jesus was proving more suc-cessful than the Baptist. This may in some measure parallel Mt 11:2-6. At any rate it would suggest that Jesus had operated as a disciple of the Baptist.

In 3:27-30 the Baptist bears his final witness to Jesus. Earlier (1:19-23) John had forcefully asserted that he was not the Messiah. Yet, he is one sent – to prepare the way of the Messiah. His role is analo-gous to that of best-man at a wedding. While acknowledging his subordinate role he rejoices in the presence of the bridegroom. 'I must decrease': John willingly departs the stage. He is one who demonstrates openness to the word of Jesus. In vv 31-36 the narra-tor adds his comment. God speaks his word of revelation through the testimony of the bridegroom, the one sent. Whoever receives the testimony of Jesus acknowledges that God is reliable, trustwor-thy. The words Jesus speaks are God's words and God is source of the measureless gift of the Spirit. In v 35 the Father's love for the Son is, for the first time, stated explicitly. It was implicit in the 'only Son' of v 16.

While revelation had been the theme of vv 31-35, the passage con-cludes with the themes of life and judgment (v 36). The believer in the Son has eternal life – a favourite Johannine theme. The Father sent Jesus and, therefore, Jesus is bearer of the divine name and authority. For us, everything depends on the stance we adopt toward him. The one who will not believe must endure 'God's wrath' – a traditional phrase. What is referred to is not a divine emotion, such as anger, but God's objective judgment that we are estranged from him through our own fault. One finds greater com-fort in Paul: 'God proves his love for us in that while we still were sinners Christ died for us' (Rom 5:8).

In the whole of 2:1-3:36 there is a response to Jesus from within Israel, the representatives of Israel being 'the Jews,' Nicodemus and the Baptist. 'Within the narrative "the word of Jesus" has been the place where the characters in the story encounter what God is doing in and through Jesus. By this criterion "the Jews" demonstrate a total lack of faith while the faith of Nicodemus is limited by his determination to understand Jesus by his own categories. Finally, John the Baptist sees himself as friend of the bridegroom, rejoicing to hear his voice. He shows an openness to the word of Jesus, cost what it may: "he must increase but I must decrease".'9

The Samaritan Woman (4:1-54)

In chapters 2-3 there were responses to Jesus from within Israel. The encounter with the Samaritan woman is a response from outside Israel. Notably, v 4 states that 'he had to go through Samaria'. Jesus' move beyond Israel followed a divine design. The fourth gospel is a gospel of personal relationships. Jesus speaks of his own relationship with his Father, with disciples and of the relationship of disciples among themselves (e.g. 15:1-17). He also reveals himself in relationship with individuals, for example, with Nicodemus (ch 3), with a blind man (ch 9) and, here, with a Samaritan woman. He takes the initiative in revealing himself while they discover who he is and what he means to them. Our passage is an invitation to faith.

A weary Jesus sat by a well in hostile Samaria – a rare glimpse of his vulnerable humanness. 'How is it that you, a Jew, ask of me, a woman of Samaria?' – a world of meaning crammed into a single question. Why this breach of convention that a man should so casually address a lone woman? The disciples, later, could not hide their scandal at such conduct: 'They were astonished that he was speaking with a woman' (v 27). And a Jew ought to know better than to ask a favour of a Samaritan! But the woman had spoken in reply to Jesus' request for a drink, and a dialogue was afoot. In a striking switch, Jesus moved from asking the woman for a drink of water to offering her a drink (v 10).

The woman, intrigued by Jesus' offer of 'living water', forgot her antagonism and spoke to him again. He had offered fresh water – where is that flowing spring? The 'Jew' of v 9 has become 'Sir' (v 11); she suggests (ironically no doubt) that he may be greater than 'our father Jacob.' The 'living water' theme exemplifies the Johannine technique of double-expression: a word of Jesus is taken by his interlocutor at its first, superficial, level; Jesus then goes on to draw out its deeper meaning. Here he explained that he was not offering spring water but life-giving water that is gift of God. It is the word of revelation which becomes a life-giving spring within the believer. The woman – though she did not really understand – was open to Jesus' offer: a necessary aspect of faith.

When Jesus disclosed his awareness of her marital record the woman saluted him as a 'prophet' – she already had come a long way. He then spoke to her of the new age when true worship will no longer be that of Garizim (the Samaritan holy mountain) or of Jerusalem. Jesus himself will be the temple, the focus of worship 'in spirit and truth' – Jesus reveals a God and Father who is to be worshipped with total commitment. God seeks such worshippers. The woman expressed her hope in a Messiah who would show her all that Jesus had been telling her. Jesus acknowledged that he was that Messiah (v 26). 'I am' (*egó eimi*) recalls Ex 3:14 and echoes Is 43:10; 45:18 where it refers to the living presence of God among his people. For John, Jesus as the 'one sent' is that presence. The woman went in haste to tell her people that she had met with the Messiah (see v 29). But she had understood only at the level of her traditional expectation. Still, there had been progress. At first, Jesus was 'a Jew', then, more respectfully, 'Sir'. The suspicion that he might be 'greater than our father Jacob' introduced a new note. Rapidly, he was 'prophet' and, finally, 'Messiah'. The narrative has been of a coming to faith, albeit imperfect faith. Perhaps we, Christians, can still identify with the woman. We need to grow in our understanding of Jesus. To let him into our lives can be embarrassing. His light shows up what is within us, lighting areas we would prefer to leave in the dark. Above all, we learn that we know him by personal encounter and that we can have from him the water of life.

The disciples, who had gone to buy food, were *scandalised* to find Jesus talking with a woman – *solus cum sola*! Already that sad – disastrous – Christian obsession with sex, to the consistent devaluation of women. As a male Christian I make no secret of my conviction that it will be only when my sisters reach whole equality in the household of the faith that I can recognise the church as truly the *ekklésia* of Jesus Christ. I accept that I will go to my grave without witnessing that goal. I can live with myself because I have the vision and am confident that it will be. 'Food' is a typically Johannine double expression and the disciples misunderstood. The 'food' of Jesus is to do the Father's will, to complete his work. He does so as the 'one sent' (see 1:14, 18, 34; 2:16; 3:16-17, 35-36). And, seeing the Samaritans (alerted by the woman's story) thronging to him, he described his mission as 'harvest' (vv 35-38); the Samaritans are already ripe for harvesting. The disciples were sent to continue the missionary labour already initiated by the Baptist and Jesus (v 38). Many of the Samaritans had believed on the testimony of the woman, sharing her partial faith. They came to a deeper faith as they heard his word, as they encountered Jesus. Now they 'know' him to be the universal Saviour. They have reached authentic faith: they have believed because of the word of Jesus. The whole passage turns out to be a sophisticated catechesis on the origin and growth of Christian faith.

> With 'the word' of Jesus as the criterion, the story of Jesus' presence among the Samaritans points to the possibility of no faith (vv 1-15: the Samaritan woman), partial faith (vv 16-30: the Samaritan woman), and authentic Johannine belief (vv 39-42: the Samaritan villagers in the world beyond the boundaries of Judaism).[10]

The Second Cana Miracle (4:46-54)

The healing of the official's son is a variant of the synoptic story of the healing of the centurion's servant (Mt 8:5-13; Lk 7:1-10). Jesus crossed from Samaria to Galilee and came to Cana; the reader is reminded of the 'sign' that Jesus had formerly worked there. The 'royal official' (4:46) was, most likely, a Gentile. 'Unless you see signs and wonders you will not believe' (v 48) – again the question of partial or authentic faith is introduced. As at 2:5, a rebuke was ignored (v 49). The man 'believed the word' of Jesus, the assurance that his son would live (v 50). He had believed; he came to 'know' that the word was efficacious. Compare 4:42 – the Samaritans 'believed' and 'knew'. The man's household believed along with him. A community of believers had come into being (v 53).

Chapters 2 to 4 of John have to do with coming to faith in Jesus. The criterion is in 2:1-11: the mother of Jesus believed in the word of her Son (2:5); Jesus manifested his 'glory' and the disciples believed (2:11). This is the yardstick which measures responses to Jesus from within Judaism (2:13-3:36) and from without (ch 4). Also, in these chapters, the Prologue's promise of the lifegiving power that comes from 'believing' and 'receiving' the Word made flesh is played out in the story of Jesus as people come to accept his word.

The Prologue introduced a Word eternally present with God and now spoken into our world. That Word became flesh in Jesus. He is, henceforth, revelation of God – that revelation, his 'glory'. There is a greater gift than torah, God's word of old. The Son knows the Father and has made him known. The Baptist pointed to Jesus as Lamb of God and the Son of God. Others acknowledged him to be Messiah and King of Israel. These are titles within the perspective of Jewish messianic hope. Jesus presented himself as Son of Man, the way of communication between God and the world.

Enter the first believer, in the Johannine understanding of faith. 'Do whatever he tells you': the mother of Jesus had placed total trust in his word. Jesus' first 'sign' was a manifestation of himself as Revealer – the symbol, his copious gift of wine. The water at the wedding had been 'for the Jewish rites of purification'; the old order had been replaced. This is underwritten in the cleansing of the temple. The temple, too, will cease to be. The risen Lord will henceforth be the dwelling place of God.

In dialogue with 'a leader of the Jews' Jesus spoke of new birth, from above, birth to eternal life. This will be when the Son of Man had been 'lifted up' in death. His death is the supreme moment of the revelation of God's love: the sending of his Son for the salvation of the world. The Baptist reappeared to voice his final testimony to Jesus. Then he bowed, gracefully, from the stage.

* * *

Following on a series of responses from within Israel came responses from without: from a Samaritan woman and Samaritan villagers. The lively story of encounter with the woman is a catechesis on the growth of faith. From the first hostile 'a Jew', the woman progressed to 'Sir', 'greater than Jacob', 'prophet', 'Messiah'. But, in the story, she did not reach full faith. The Samaritan villagers first came to believe in Jesus 'because of the woman's testimony.' They attained full faith in 'the Saviour of the world' on the basis of his word. With the second Cana miracle and the faith of a household, a community of believers had come into being. As the Prologue had promised, those who believed in and received the Word-made-flesh became children of God.

CHAPTER 4

Jesus and the Feasts

I am the bread of life ... I am the light of the world ...
I am the good shepherd (Jn 6:35; 8:12; 10:11)

The climax of the Jewish War of 68-70 AD, the destruction of Jerusalem and the temple, and the near obliteration of Judaism, was traumatic not only for Jews but for Christians and, in particular, Jewish-Christians. As a Jewish Christian, writing out of and for a Jewish Christian community, Matthew, like all Jews, had to face up to a radical challenge to Jewish identity. There were stark questions: Where is Israel now? Who is heir to the biblical promises? The gospel of Matthew is a Jewish-Christian answer.[11] We find a parallel situation in the fourth gospel. With the destruction of the temple Judaism had to turn, exclusively, to synagogue-centred worship. Jews had to rethink their celebration of the traditional, temple-centred, feasts. Johannine Christians, expelled from the synagogue, and without access to their traditional feasts, had to develop their own way of access to God. This is why John 5-10 is dominated by Jewish feasts. More accurately: it is dominated by Jesus' replacement of Jewish feasts. In 5:1 Jesus went to Jerusalem to be present at 'a feast of the Jews'. Subsequently he would be present at Passover (ch 6), Tabernacles (7:1-10:21) and Dedication (10:22-42). What emerges is that, in practice, Jesus was replacing each feast. He is the new focus of worship (see 2:21; 4:21-23).

JESUS AND THE SABBATH (5:1-47)

After the events in Galilee (from Cana to Cana) Jesus went to Jerusalem because 'there was a festival of the Jews' (5:1). The feast is unspecified. The key is in v 9b – 'Now that day was a sabbath' – sabbath is the centre of this chapter. The vague 'a festival of the Jews' is, in some sort, a pointer to the issue throughout chapters 5-10.

Healing on a Sabbath (5:1-18)

In Jerusalem, by the pool of Bethzatha, Jesus happened upon a man who had been a cripple for thirty-eight years. He had been by the pool for a long time hoping, in vain, for healing. Jesus healed him. He picked up his sleeping-mat and walked off. It was sabbath. By carrying a 'load', his sleeping-mat, the man was infringing a sabbath rule and was duly challenged by 'the Jews'. His excuse was that he had been told to do so by the one who had healed him – one whose name he did not know. Later Jesus met him in the temple. The man went and told the Jews that it was Jesus who had healed him. Thereupon 'the Jews started persecuting Jesus because he was doing such things on the sabbath' (v 16).

Jesus' response was: 'My Father is still working, and I also am still working' (v 17). Despite Gen 2:2-3 ('God rested from all the work he had done') Jewish theologians were satisfied that God could never 'rest' – he could never cease to be active, not even on the sabbath; otherwise creation would cease to be. Here, Jesus refers to God as Father in a provocative sense. He does this work (healing) on the sabbath just as his Father works also on the sabbath. Surely he is usurping a divine prerogative and so 'making himself equal to God!' (v 18). This charge is likely a Jewish misunderstanding of Johannine Christian claims for Jesus. But John does not make Jesus equal to God as is clear in the sequel (vv 19-30).

Life and Judgment (5:19-30)

The activity of the Son is twofold: giving life and judging. As the one sent 'the Son can do nothing on his own' (v 19). Jesus is apprentice to his Father; all he does he has learned from him (v 20). As that son-apprentice, the Son can give life as the Father gives life and can judge as the Father judges. To honour the Son, then, is to honour the Father. To hear the word of the Son is to hear the Father and gain eternal life. The one who hears the word of Jesus and trusts in the Father who sent Jesus, has already passed from death to life. The Father is Judge; he has passed on to the Son the authority of judgment. In the Johannine view, however, judgment is auto-judgment – one turns from the light. Verse 30, 'I can do nothing on my own' catches up v 19, 'the Son can do nothing on his own.' This underlines the status of the Son as the one sent. He is the one who wholly represents the Father and speaks fully in his name.

In vv 31-47 the discourse moves on to the issue of testimony to
Jesus. The question of 'witnesses' shifts the language of judging
from judgment passed on others to that which others pass on Jesus.
Jesus defends himself. He needs witnesses on his behalf – the 'two
or three witnesses' required by the Law (Deut 19:15). He has form-
idable witnesses. The Father had borne witness to him through the
testimony of John the Baptist. The works of Jesus testified on his
behalf because they had been wrought by the Father through him.
The scriptures bore witness – scripture is word of God. The Jews
were proud of their knowledge of scripture; that pride was their
undoing. Their disbelief was culpable. They did not 'love God', did
not respond to God and serve his interests – they were too
engrossed in self-interest. Jesus would not be their accuser.
Ironically, their accuser would be the very Moses in whom they had
placed their hope! If they had really understood their Moses they
would have discerned the continuity between the writings of
Moses and the words of Jesus. In the event, he who should have
been their advocate will be their prosecutor.

JESUS AND THE PASSOVER (CH 6)

The Feeding (6:1-15)

All four gospels carry the story of the multiplication of loaves. Mark
(6:32-44; 8:1-10) and Matthew (14:13-21; 15:29-38) have two
accounts of a miraculous feeding. There are solid arguments for
regarding these two accounts in Matthew and Mark as variant
forms of the same incident. And it seems best to take it that the
fourth evangelist (Jn 6:1-15) drew on an independent tradition quite
like that of Mark's and Matthew's second account.

The introductory sentences (Jn 6:1-3) bring together motifs which
belong to the common substance of the gospel tradition: a journey
across the lake, the pressure of the crowd, the reputation of Jesus as
healer, his withdrawal to the 'mountain' with his disciples. In v 4
we meet a distinctively Johannine trait: 'Now the Passover, the festival of the Jews, was near' – note, festival of the Jews. Passover is
the essential background of this chapter. The language of vv 10-12
recalls a eucharistic celebration: Jesus took the loaves, gave thanks
and distributed them. While in the synoptic gospels the disciples

distributed the bread, John has Jesus himself do it – reminiscent of the Last Supper. Only in John is the gathering of fragments given as a command of Jesus. In the *Didache* the same word, *synagein*, is used of gathering for eucharist. The people discerned a 'sign' (v 14) but were not led beyond elementary faith. It seemed to them that Jesus was the prophet-like-Moses (see Deut 18:15-18) of popular expectation. A parallel hope was of a second gift of manna to mark the messianic age (see 2 Bar 29:8). The crowd's further view of him as king was rejected by Jesus as he retired from the scene. He is God's spokesman and true Messiah – but not as understood by his contemporaries. Christians must beware that our understanding of Christ is not tainted with triumphalism.

The incident of walking on the waters (vv 16-21) is closely connected with the feeding of the five thousand also in the synoptics (Mk 6:45-52; Mt 14:22-23). Evidently, a traditional association. The appearance of Jesus on the waters is reminiscent of a prerogative of Yahweh (see Job 9:8; 77:19). Jesus declared 'I am' (*egó eimi*), claiming to be much more than the political messiah the crowd had thought him to be.

Discourse on the Bread from Heaven (6:25-29)

This discourse is a homily on the text in v 31 – 'He gave them bread from heaven to eat.' It is interspersed with questions (vv 25, 30, 34, 41, 52) to which Jesus responds. Verses 25-29 are an introduction. The crowd had seen the 'sign' but that had not touched them at any deep level. Jesus accused them of seeking him simply because they had enjoyed a free meal. In v 27 he began to press his message home in terms of familiar Johannine dualism: perishable food and the food of eternal life. That abiding food ought to be the object of their striving. There is an implicit contrast with the Law: in Jewish tradition it was life-giving (see Sir 17:11; 45:5). Jesus offered a better source of life. The crowd wanted to know what they should do to please God ('to perform the works of God'). What pleases God is to believe in Jesus, the one 'whom he has sent.' They questioned Jesus' claims. They had seen in him the prophet-like-Moses; now they challenged him to provide manna: a sign of the end-time. Jesus' reply was that it was not Moses who gave the bread from heaven; it is the Father who gives the genuine (*aléthinos*) heavenly bread. The true bread from heaven is Jesus. The crowd misunderstood.

Jesus, Bread of Life (6:35-51)

Jesus made a formal declaration: 'I am the bread of life.' This is not a statement of who Jesus is but of what he does: he feeds with life-giving bread. Those given by the Father come to Jesus in faith. He, on his part, welcomes all who come to him and will drive no one away. He acts so because, as the one sent, he responds, without question, to the will of the Father. Not one of those who, given by the Father, come to him, will be lost. See 18:9. All who come to believe in the Son will have life, now and forever.

Up to this, Jesus had dialogued with 'the crowd'; now, at v 41, the crowd suddenly becomes 'the Jews'. They 'murmured' like the Israelites in the wilderness (see Ex 15:24; 16:2, 7). They challenged his claim to be bread from heaven. They think they know him – son of Joseph, his parents well known. But he had been sent by God from God and those who believe in him are those whom the Father draws to him. His word is word of God. Whoever had listened to him had been taught by the Father. The bread from heaven is revelation of the Father, in the person and through the words of Jesus. True, Moses had referred to the manna as bread from heaven (see Ex 16:15). Jesus insisted that he is the living bread from heaven. And he elaborated: 'The bread that I will give for the life of the world is my flesh' (v 51).

My Flesh is Food Indeed (6:52-59)

If Jesus is both the bread and the giver of bread, then what he gives is himself: his flesh and blood. 'The Jews', as is to be expected, misunderstood Jesus' promise of the bread that is flesh – his very self. Jesus, in turn, became more explicit: whoever eats the flesh and drinks the blood of him, the Son of Man, has eternal life. 'Flesh' points to the human reality of Jesus; 'blood' points to the reality of his death. The total gift of himself involves, for Jesus, the breaking of his body and the shedding of his blood. It is the gift of his whole self for the life of the world. The death of Jesus is the ultimate revelation of God – who 'did not spare his own Son'; who did not shrink from human rejection of himself in the rejection of the Son.

To believe in Jesus is to eat and drink: he is indeed food and drink in that he gives and sustains life. He is living bread; he bestows life on

those who accept his revelation of a living Father. 'To eat' Jesus is
'to believe' in him. It is a powerful way of stressing the reality of
authentic faith and the object of that faith: the Son and his saving
death.

> The discourse, from v 25 down to v 59, presents Jesus as the true
> bread from heaven, replacing the former bread from heaven, the
> manna of the Law. The believer must accept the revelation of
> God that will take place in broken flesh and spilled blood (vv 53-
> 54) ... But at the end of the first century Johannine Christians,
> and the Christian readers of subsequent centuries, have every
> right to ask: where do we encounter this revelation of God in the
> flesh and blood of the Son of Man? The author's insinuation of
> eucharistic language into the final section of the discourse pro-
> vides the answer: one encounters the flesh and blood of Jesus
> Christ in eucharistic celebration.[12]

Crisis (6:60-71)

It should not surprise that 'the Jews' could not accept the word of
Jesus. Now we learn that 'many of his disciples' would no longer
listen to his word (vv 60-66). They failed to do so because they were
operating by human standards – according to 'the flesh'. Here *sarx*
('flesh') is taken in the sense of the merely human (see 3:6). In contrast, the *sarx* of Jesus is of the Word-made-flesh (1:14) and is life-
giving (ch 6). It is this distinction that explains the seeming contradiction between the positive meaning of 'flesh' in vv 51-58 (the flesh
of Jesus) and the statement 'the flesh is useless' in v 63.

What, then, does v 63 mean? ('It is the spirit that gives life; the flesh
is useless. The words that I have spoken to you are spirit and life.')
Noteworthy is the reappearance of *pneuma* ('spirit'). In the Nicodemus passage (3:1-10) we are told that the realm of 'the above' is
the sphere of 'spirit' and that rebirth into the eternal life of the higher
realm is birth 'of the Spirit' (3:3-8). And there is the forceful statement, 'What is born of the flesh is flesh, and what is born of the
Spirit is spirit' (v 6). Similarly here (6:63) the point is made that only
one 'born of the Spirit' can accept that Jesus has come from heaven
and can receive his revelation. One 'born of the flesh', and so open
only to the merely human, cannot know him or his teaching.
'Because of this many of his disciples turned back and no longer

went about with him' (v 66). This, surely, reflects a Johannine community experience. Some Johannine Christians had left in protest at the high christology elaborated in the community.

In v 67 Jesus challenged the twelve: Will they, too, desert him? Peter assured him that Jesus, and only he, can be the centre of their lives: 'you have the words of eternal life' – an echo of Jesus' words in v 63. Peter was sure that Jesus is 'the Holy One of God'. The twelve had come 'to believe and to know': they had attained full Johannine faith. It was at a price. The chapter ends on a sombre note (vv 70-71): Jesus, Bread of Life – the life-giver – will be brought to death by unbelief and betrayal.

The fact that disciples leave Jesus on account of his word, that the twelve make a fine confession of faith through the words of Simon Peter, and then that one of the twelve is singled out as the future betrayer, reflects the tension that the Johannine perspective created for people in the community. Even 'insiders' were not able to stay with the community as it developed its exalted theological and christological story of Jesus.[13]

JESUS AND THE TABERNACLES (7:1-10:21)

The feast of Tabernacles is the background for 7:1-10:21. The Hebrew *sukkot* is variously translated: Tabernacles, Booths, Tents, Shelters. It was celebrated in autumn, in the seventh month (Sept-Oct). It was originally a seven-day festival to which an eighth was added. Of the annual pilgrimage feasts this was the best attended. Josephus referred to it as 'the holiest and greatest of Hebrew feasts'. Two of its ceremonies are of immediate relevance here: water libation and light. Each morning a procession, led by priests, brought water from the pool of Siloam. It was taken to the temple and poured over the altar. Jewish tradition linked the Messiah with the gift of water. Four menorahs (the seven-branched lampstands) were set up in the centre of the court of the women. They lighted up the night.

At the Feast (7:1-36)

Opposition to Jesus had hardened and had begun to mobilise. Jesus decided to remain in Galilee for some time; 'the Jews' were planning to kill him if he moved into Judea. His brothers (last mentioned at 2:12) urged him to go with them to Jerusalem for the feast of Tabernacles – where he might display his works. He told them to go by themselves; his hour for 'going up' was not yet. Later he did, on his own and quietly, go to Jerusalem. The Jews had sought him and were disappointed that he had not shown up: 'Where is he?' He was being discussed. Some of the people were on Jesus' side; others thought he was a heretic. This is a reflection of debates over Jesus between Johannine Christians and their opponents.

Half-way through the week-long feast Jesus began to teach openly in the temple. There was surprise on the part of the Jews: where did he get his theological learning? The basic issue was one of authority: is God revealed in Jewish tradition or in Jesus' teaching? Jesus responded that he had his teaching from him who had sent him. People of good will would readily discern the source of his teaching. He accused 'the Jews' of self-interest and of seeking to kill him. They had criticised Jesus for healing on the sabbath (see 5:2-18). They themselves had no problem with performing circumcision on the sabbath. What, then, was wrong with Jesus' 'healing a man's whole body'?

Some of the people were surprised that Jesus had appeared openly; they knew that 'the Jews' were seeking to kill him. Perhaps the authorities had come to accept that Jesus was the Messiah after all? On the other hand, the Messiah would remain hidden until his spectacular appearance (a popular notion). But all knew that Jesus was from Nazareth. Johannine irony: they do not know the true provenance of Jesus. He informed them that he was from the one who had sent him – the one whom they did not know. 'The Jews' understood that he was, again, referring to his Father. They would have arrested him, but it was not yet his 'hour.' Some did believe that Jesus was the Messiah. Their belief fell short of Johannine faith (vv 25-31). The priests and Pharisees had not given in; they sent temple police to arrest him. Jesus told his opponents that he would soon return to him who had sent him. They would seek him in vain, for they could not follow him. They surmised: was he going to the diaspora, outside their control? (vv 32-36).

On the Last Day of the Feast (7:37-8:59)

The last day of the festival was the eighth. The water and light ceremonies had ended on the previous seventh day. Jesus now proclaimed that he was giver of water (vv 37-38) and light of the world
(8:12). This eighth day is, truly, 'the great day' (v 37).

Jesus made a solemn proclamation:
    Let anyone who is thirsty come to me,
    and let the one who believes in me drink.
    As the scripture has said, 'Out of his heart
    shall flow rivers of living water' (vv 37-38).

In Ezek 47:1-12 lifegiving waters flowed from the temple. Jesus
declared that lifegiving water flowed from him; his person is now
the source of living water. He spoke of the Spirit, the powerful presence of God. 'As yet there was no Spirit' (v 39), the Spirit would not
be until Jesus had been 'glorified'. The risen Christ will give the
Spirit (see 20:22). Only when manifested ('glorified') on the cross
will he be wholly the dispenser of God's power (vv 37-39).

Questions about Jesus' identity persisted. The crowd was divided.
Some, though they had not understood, were impressed: here was
the prophet-like-Moses – perhaps even the Messiah! Others objected
that the Messiah would come from Bethlehem, village of David;
Jesus was a Galilean. The origin of Jesus had them well and truly
puzzled (vv 40-41). The authorities had sent temple police to arrest
Jesus (v 32). These returned to the chief priests and Pharisees,
empty-handed. When asked why they had failed to arrest him they
could only answer that never had they heard anyone speak as Jesus
had spoken. The annoyed Pharisees retorted that the authorities
were not so gullible; only the accursed rabble who knew nothing of
the Law could be deceived. Nicodemus protested: Surely the Law
expects us to grant a fair hearing before we condemn? He got short
shrift. With heavy sarcasm he was asked, Are you a Galilean too?
You are supposed to know your scripture; then you must know that
prophets do not come from Galilee! One thing had become clear:
Jesus' enemies might not know what to make of him, but they were
grimly set on getting rid of him (vv 45-52).

The Light of the World (8:12-30)

The ceremony of light had concluded. On this last day of Tabernacles Jesus declared: 'I am the light of the world' (v 12). As light of the world (1:9) his coming had divided humanity into those who 'come to the light' and those whose 'evil deeds' led them to choose darkness (3:19-21). Jesus had replaced the light ceremonies of Tabernacles as he had previously replaced its water ritual. He was the light: whoever would follow him would walk in the light of life. The Pharisees objected that his self-witness was not valid; that, in fact, he lied. Jesus emphatically asserted that his testimony was true and valid. He knew whence he came and where he was going. They did not know and were in no position to pass judgment on him. They judged by human standards, and condemned him. He was not in the business of condemning anyone. To the question, 'Where is your Father?' he retorted that if they knew him they would know the Father. As it was, they knew neither Son nor Father. He continued to teach openly and was not arrested, 'because his hour had not yet come' (vv 12-20).

Jesus told his opponents that he was going where they could not come (see 7:33-36). They wondered aloud whether he intended to commit suicide! He and they belonged to two different worlds. He had come into their world to empower them to be begotten from above. To attain that eternal life they must believe Jesus' assertion: I AM (*egó eimi*). They must believe that he possessed the lifegiving power of the Father. Throughout Second Isaiah (see 41:4; 43:10,13; 45:18; 46:4; 48:12) the expression 'I am' is used to present Yahweh as the unique God of Israel, and as the only God. By using the same formula Jesus makes the unique claim to be the presence of God to humankind. He drove the matter home: 'When you have lifted up the Son of Man, then you will realise that I AM' (v 28). They may crucify him ('lift up'); indeed, they will. But that 'lifting up' will be his revelation of God. It is because he is one with the Father, the Sent One who wholly represents the Father, that Jesus can speak his I AM. Jesus is unique revelation of God (vv 21-30).

Jesus went on to tell 'the Jews' that the truth would set them free – meaning that he was truth, embodying the Father's saving purpose. They retorted that they stood in no need of being set free: they were free children of Abraham. Jesus rejoined that they were slaves,

slaves of sin. He, the Son, could set them free. As for being children of Abraham, why then did they want to kill him? That was not to act as Abraham's children. In fact, they were doing the work of their father. They protested, 'God is our father!' Jesus replied that, if it were so, they would love him, the Son. But, 'you are from your father the devil' (v 44). They prove it because they turn from the truth and embrace lies. Could any of them convict Jesus of sin, of turning from God's purpose? If they were from God they would have hearkened to the word of God that he had spoken. In the Johannine view people have to be 'of God' or 'not of God' (vv 31-47).

'The Jews' counter-attacked: Jesus is 'Samaritan', 'Madman'. A lively dialogue ensued. He retorted: 'I am not mad. I know my Father; I do not seek self-glory. The Father, the life-giver, is the one who glorifies me. And I tell you most solemnly, whoever keeps my word will never see death.' They shot back: 'now there is no doubt; you are crazy! Are you greater than the prophets, greater than our father Abraham? They have tasted death, and you declare: "Whoever keeps my word will never see death." Who do you claim to be?' Jesus answered: 'I tell you: your father Abraham rejoiced that he was to see my coming (the age to come had been revealed to him by God); he saw it and was glad.' They retorted: 'You have seen Abraham – you, not yet fifty! You are quite mad!' Jesus fired his parting shot: 'I assure you: before Abraham was I AM' – the one who bears God's name and wields his power. The claim was blasphemy to them. They attempted to stone him, but he left the temple and slipped away. The rift was complete. (vv 48-59)

EXCURSUS: THE WOMAN TAKEN IN ADULTERY (8:1-11)

This passage – The woman taken in adultery – is not in context in the fourth gospel, while in form and style it closely resembles the synoptic tradition. It is quite in the style of Luke. It seems to have been inserted in John because of the reference, in 7:51, to judgment according to the Law.

The purpose of the scribes and Pharisees in bringing the adulteress to Jesus was to entrap him. If he pardoned her he could be accused of encouraging people to infringe the Law of Moses which prescribed death by stoning for such conduct (Lev 20:10; Deut 13:9-10). In fact, as the Wisdom literature makes clear, that grim prescription had long been a dead letter, but the Law could still be invoked as a challenge to Jesus. On the other hand, if he would agree that she should be stoned to death, he would lose his name for mercy. Jesus deftly turned the challenge: let the woman's accusers look to their own sins! He will not be judge. Although the Father had given full authority to his Son to pass judgment (Jn 5:22) Jesus really judges no one (8:15). His message is of mercy and forgiveness.

The story ends with the quiet scene of reconciliation between Jesus and the woman. The accusers had gone; Jesus alone remained to proclaim to her God's mercy. Augustine comments: *relicti sunt duo – misera et misericordia*: two stood there alone – wretchedness and mercy.

HEALING OF A MAN BORN BLIND (CH 9)

Like the episode of the Samaritan woman (ch 4) this splendid story is, too, a lesson on growth in faith. The miracle of the granting of sight to a blind man is a 'sign'. Jesus thereby reveals that he is 'the light of the world' (v 5) – still the Tabernacles setting. In giving physical sight, Jesus demonstrated that by his teaching, life and personal presence he was the source of the spiritual vision we call believing. The whole account reads like a picturesque, symbolic presentation of the manner in which one comes to believe in Jesus as 'Lord'. Healed quickly of his physical disability, the man was the subject of a gradual illumination ('the man called Jesus', 'a prophet', 'a man from God') until, finally, he came to faith: 'Lord, I believe' (v 38).

An Old Testament view (firmly endorsed by Job's theologian 'comforters') saw a necessary link between affliction and sin; Jesus rejected any such necessary connection (vv 1-3). The man was bidden to wash in the pool of Siloam (Tabernacles association) –'which means sent'. This is a play on the name Siloam; in the context reference is to 'the One Sent.' 'He came back, able to see.' Yet, the cure was really achieved not by the waters of Siloam but by the Sent One. His neighbours and those who recognised the beggar wanted to know how it happened that he was now sighted. He told them that the one who had healed him was 'the man called Jesus'. It happened to be a sabbath. The Pharisees considered Jesus' making of the paste he spread on the patient's eyes to be 'work' and so an infringement of sabbath observance (vv 6-7, 14). Some immediately concluded that Jesus, as one who did not honour the sabbath, could not be from God. Others were not so sure: could a sinner give sight to the blind? As often in John, a 'division' (*schisma*) occurred. The man who earlier had referred to 'the man called Jesus' now stated his deeper conviction: 'He is a prophet' (vv 1-17).

The Pharisees – now become 'the Jews' – called the parents to account. They acknowledged that their son was born blind. They have no idea how it is he now sees. And they will not get involved. The fear of the parents (v 22) and the *de facto* expulsion of their son (v 34) reflect a time when one could no longer profess faith in Jesus Christ and remain within the community of Israel. At first, Jewish Christians had been tolerated by their fellow Jews. In the Johannine situation the matter was exacerbated by the distinctive Johannine christology (vv 18-23).

'The Jews' then attempted to proclaim Jesus a sinner and questioned the man again. They reviled him for his claim that Jesus is from God. They adjured the man: 'Give glory to God' – a formula used when people are to confess their guilt. He insisted that Jesus had healed his blindness – scarcely the deed of a sinner (it could only have been God's achievement, through Jesus). As they pressed their questioning he observed, sarcastically, that they seemed so interested in Jesus that they must be thinking of becoming his disciples! Angrily, they retorted: 'We are disciples of Moses – and God spoke to Moses. But who knows where this fellow comes from.' This exchange set the man among the 'disciples of Jesus' and the Jews as 'disciples of Moses'. Again, a later conflict situation between Christian community and synagogue. The man would not be browbeaten: 'You do not know where he comes from, and he has opened my eyes! This has never happened before; of course he is from God!' The man's faith grew as he stoutly defended Jesus. He became more and more convinced that Jesus was from God (the one sent). Sadly, while the blind man opened more and more to the light, the Pharisees, though physically sighted, were spiritually blind. The man was driven from the synagogue. It was the experience of Johannine Christians who had been similarly expelled (vv 24-34).

The man was ready for a further step on his faith journey. Jesus encountered him and issued the challenge: 'Do you believe in the Son of Man?' With charming directness he replied: 'Sir, tell me who he is that I may believe.' Convinced that he had seen the Son and had heard his word, he made his profession, 'Lord, I believe!' and fell on his knees in acknowledgment of the God-sent bringer of salvation. He had advanced from his Jewish belief (vv 31-33) to Christian faith. Yet, there remain those who would not believe (vv 39-41). The blind man could not 'see' in the manner of the Pharisees with their vaunted knowledge of the Law and of the ways of God, but he was open and could come to faith. Those who could 'see' were blinded by that puny light which held their gaze and could not perceive the Light of the world (vv 35-41).

JESUS, GOOD SHEPHERD (10:1-21).

Against the background of Ezekiel 34, Jesus presented himself as the 'shepherd' of God's flock and the 'door' of access to God. In a Palestinian setting the sheepfold was a courtyard or a walled enclosure in a field. At night the sheep of various shepherds were gathered within. There was a proper manner of approaching sheep herded in a sheepfold: through the gate opened by the keeper. Any other mode of entry was conduct of a thief. Then there is the shepherd. He knows his sheep by name; when he calls them they follow him confidently. They will not follow a stranger; they do not recognise his voice. The parabolic form wears thin as Jesus reveals his own part in the picture. It is because the parable is really about him that the same person can fill the role of shepherd, and also of gate giving access to the fold. The Lord not only gives and sustains life but is himself the way, or means of entry, into life. As the good shepherd, Jesus contrasted himself with the Pharisees who had just expelled from the synagogue the man born blind (9:34). (What does Jesus think of the hounding of theologians in our day?). Jesus 'leads out' and 'goes ahead of' his sheep as their leader and guides them to the pasturage of his word. And he calls each 'by name' – there is a close personal relationship between the Christian and Christ.

Jesus also described himself as the gate of the sheepfold; he is the way of life (see 14:6). In and through him alone do Christians enter into 'life' – a gift bestowed with lavish generosity. Here there is the same loving care as before and the same intimate familiarity – they 'go in and go out' as they please. While Jesus spoke of himself as shepherd and way, the passage must be a challenge to all who hold pastoral responsibility. They will do well to contemplate the picture of caring vigilance and patient love that the good shepherd presents, and mark his respect for the freedom of his disciples (vv 1-10).

Jesus declared himself to be the good or ideal shepherd. Again, Ezekiel 34 is the background. God promises his people, in the first place, that he would become their shepherd, and then that he would choose a shepherd for them in the messianic age. Jesus' assertion that he was the good shepherd indicates that this age has come, and that he is that promised shepherd. He is a shepherd so very different from those castigated by Ezekiel: 'You have not strengthened the weak, you have not healed the sick, you have not bound up the injured, you have not brought back the strayed, you have not sought the lost, but with force and harshness you have ruled them' (Ezek 34:4). On every point he stood in sharp contrast.

The second characteristic of the true shepherd is that he knows his sheep intimately and that they know him. In John the mutual knowledge of Jesus and those who belong to him is an extension of the mutual knowledge of Father and Son (see Jn 17:26-27). Knowing Jesus and the Father means being of one mind and heart with them. But the shepherd concern of Jesus reached out to other sheep – the Gentiles – to bring them also into the fold of eternal life. Jesus declared that the Father loved him because he was prepared to sacrifice life itself in faithfulness to the task entrusted to him. Because he was so fully one with the Father, source of life and life-giver, he had power not only to lay down his life, but power to take it up again. 'I have received this command from my Father'; as always in John, it is the Father who initiates activity (v 11-18).

Jesus (vv 17-18) spoke of laying down life:

> Death is often seen as making a mockery of life, love, and freedom, but when Jesus speaks of his own death, he sees it otherwise. Having said earlier that the Father's love for the Son is expressed in showing him how to create and give life (5:19-21), he now states that this Father's love is particularly expressed in Jesus' dying: 'Because of this the Father loves me, that I lay

down my life, in order that I may take it up again.' It is not that
the Father's love is dependent on Jesus' death. Rather, that love
is presupposed; but in Jesus' dying the Father's love is expressed
in a special way and is grounded yet more firmly.[14]

'The Jews' did not know what to make of Jesus' words – again a
'division' *(schisma)*. Some declared flatly: 'He's a raving lunatic.'
Others observed more thoughtfully: 'These are not the words of a
madman – and no power of evil could open the eyes of the blind'
(vv 19-21). The question of who Jesus is will not go away.

JESUS AND DEDICATION (10:22-42)

The origin of the feast of Dedication *(Hanukkah)* is described in 1
Macc 4:36-59: purification of the temple on the 25th Kisleu (Dec) 164
BC after Judas Maccabeus' successful campaign to liberate Jerusalem.
The feast lasted eight days and was marked by an atmosphere of
rejoicing. The rituals of Hanukkah were similar to those of
Tabernacles.

The passage Jn 10:22-39, in the setting of Dedication, presents Jesus
as Messiah and Son of God. The debates of Tabernacles continue.
The Messiah question is raised in v 24, 'If you are the Messiah, tells
us plainly.' Jesus responded by pointing to the works he was doing.
Verses 26-27 recall 10:1-21, the faithful sheep know the voice of
their shepherd. Verse 28 recalls the thought of the wolves who
snatch the sheep when the hireling fails to protect the flock (see
10:12). Jesus is the true shepherd and no one will snatch from his
care the sheep that the Father has given him. Note the correspon-
dence of vv 28 and 29: 'no one will snatch them out of my hand'; 'no
one can snatch them out of the Father's hand.' What comfort for the
sheep! 'The Father and I are one' (v 30): the Father and Jesus share a
oneness of purpose. In view of this, Jesus is the visible presence of
God (vv 22-30).

'The Jews' accused Jesus of 'blasphemy', usurpation of divine status
and honour. They spelled out their charge: 'You, though only a
human being, are making yourself God.' (v 33). They had misunderstood Jesus' words in v 30 ('the Father and I are one') as a claim
to be God. See 19:7. In his reply (vv 34-35) Jesus followed a Jewish
debating technique. Psalm 82:6 states: 'I say you are gods, sons of

the Most High, all of you.' The psalm castigates unjust judges. They
are called 'gods' because of their quasi-divine function (judgment
belongs to God; see Deut 1:17). Jesus' argument runs: Firstly, if
scripture can refer to human beings as 'gods,' why do the Jews
object when the term is applied to Jesus? Secondly, the judges were
called 'gods' because they were agents of God. A *fortiori*, Jesus, as
consecrated agent of the Father, deserves to be called 'god'. In short,
if those who speak in God's name are 'gods', why not Jesus who
does the work of God? In v 36 'I am God's Son' is an explanation of
the declaration 'the Father and I are one' (v 30): the Father had sent
Jesus and had given him a unique task. There is a further explanation in v 38 – 'the Father is in me and I in the Father': Father and
Son, though distinct and different, are one in a mutual sharing of
life. The debate that started at Tabernacles and ended at Dedication
closed on a tragic note (v 39). There was no longer any hope that
'the Jews' would listen to Jesus (vv 31-39).

All was not lost. Jesus went across the Jordan to where John the
Baptist had begun his mission. Had he gone because that was
where Jesus, too, had begun his mission, as disciple of the Baptist?
The move reminded some that what John had said of Jesus had
turned out to be true. These believed in him. Francis Moloney
observes that this replacement of Jewish feasts needs to be carefully
assessed. A proper understanding will aid, not confuse, Jewish-
Christian dialogue.

> The gospel does not attempt to denigrate the established and
> cherished ways of remembering and rendering present God's
> saving action among the people of Israel. The account of Jesus'
> presence at their feasts – Sabbath, Passover, Tabernacles, and
> Dedication – affirm that the former order has been perfected, not
> destroyed. The crucial difference between the two orders is the
> person of Jesus Christ. The conflict between Jesus and 'the Jews',
> as it is reported in these stories, is not a conflict between Jesus
> and Israel but rather a conflict between some from Israel who
> had definitively decided that Jesus was or was not the Christ;
> anyone who confessed he was must be put out of the synagogue
> (cf 9:22). As Jesus and 'the Jews' are on a collision course, so are
> 'the Jews' and the Johannine Christians, but the latter are proud
> to look back upon their Jewish heritage, to see in their former

festive celebrations of God in Israel the signs and shadows of the presence of Jesus among them.[15]

* * *

Jesus had spoken of his body as a new temple (2:19-21) and had told the Samaritan woman, 'the hour is coming when the true worshippers will worship the Father in spirit and truth' (4:23). Now, in chs 5-10, he is the one who replaces the sabbath and the great feasts of Judaism. He heals on a sabbath because his Father works good even on the sabbath. As Son-apprentice, he had learned everything from that Father. He does the divine works of giving life and of judging. These works, and the Father himself, are his authenticating witness.

A feeding of five thousand led to a discourse on heavenly bread, bread of life. Jesus is the bread of life, fulfilling the promise of the manna. He is the true bread given by the Father: the bread of revelation of the Father. He is 'bread' of flesh and blood: flesh as truly human, blood as one who died. His gift was of himself for the life of the world. Faith in him is the 'eating' and 'drinking' of his 'flesh and blood'. He gives and sustains life. Not all Johannine Christians could accept the high christology behind the assertions.

At Tabernacles Jesus emerged as source of the 'water of life'. As such, he is giver of the Spirit. He is the I AM: the presence of God, endowed with the lifegiving power of the Father. His full revelation of the Father is in his being 'lifted up'. The healing of the blind man was a 'sign': Jesus is light of the world. The man had walked a journey of faith, to the point where he professed, 'Lord, I believe' – and worshipped.

Jesus is Good Shepherd who knows his sheep, who lovingly cares for them, who respects their freedom. He is Gateway to Life. His sheep hear his voice and follow. No one will snatch them out of his hand. He is, truly, God's Son who does the work of his Father. The Father is God of salvation. Father and Son are at one in this purpose.

CHAPTER 5

Toward the Hour

FROM DEATH TO LIFE (11:1-54)

Jesus' raising of Lazarus is a 'sign', the most poignant sign of his life-giving mission. It is an illustration of his claim to be the resurrection and the life (11:25-26) and an indication that the 'last day' has dawned: 'Very truly, I tell you, the hour is coming, and is now here, when the dead will hear the voice of the Son of God, and those who hear will live' (5:25). As in the episode of Jesus' healing of the man born blind (ch 9), the evangelist's intention is to give a vivid pictorial presentation of the effect of believing in Jesus. There he appeared as light of the world; here he appears as life of the world. The evangelist does not want our attention to be arrested by the wonderful fact that Jesus had performed the impossible in bringing a man back to life. He wants us to see in Jesus the source of life: he is the life-giving Word of God incarnate (1:4,14). The life in question is not earthly life. The resuscitation of Lazarus is but a pointer to the life that Jesus provides.

We must understand that the resurrection which Jesus promises to those who believe in him is to be understood no more literally than the 'resurrection' of Ezekiel 37. What Jesus proclaims is that the new life of the new covenant has been given to the world in him. It is available to all who believe in him, who rely on him, and who trust in him, building their lives on his. This new life is not just a future hope. It is a present reality which physical death, despite its appearance of finality, will not negate. It is not a life merely juxtaposed to ordinary human existence, but ordinary human existence lived in a new way, in the knowledge of the one true God who has revealed himself and his plan for humankind in his Son: 'And this is eternal life, that they know you the only true God, and Jesus Christ whom you have sent' (Jn 17:3). It is knowledge of God as Father, the realisation that love is at the heart of reality, which changes existence into life.

The Raising of Lazarus (11:1-53)

Luke also (10:38-42) has the sisters Martha and Mary as friends of Jesus (he does not mention Lazarus). Now their brother Lazarus is gravely ill and the sisters send word to Jesus. Their discreet invitation, 'Lord, he whom you love is ill' is reminiscent of 2:3 – 'they have no wine'. Jesus declared that the illness would lead to his 'glorification', the revelation of God's power in the Son. His statement, 'this illness does not lead to death', means that the death of Lazarus will not be the last word. Jesus stayed where he was for two days; his actions can never be measured by human standards. See 7:8. Then he set out for Bethany, brushing aside the remonstrances of his disciples who reminded him that, last time in Jerusalem, 'the Jews' had attempted to stone him (10:31). His reason for going to Bethany was response to God's design. He told his disciples bluntly that Lazarus was dead. He was 'glad' for their sake because they would receive a new stimulus for their faith. Thomas misunderstood; Jesus sought their belief, not their death. Jesus knew that he would call Lazarus to life, though his life-giving would cost him his own life (vv 1-16).

On arrival at Bethany he found that Lazarus had been buried four days earlier. When she was told that he had reached the village, Martha came to meet him; Mary stayed at home. The sisters display the same temperaments as in Lk 10:38-41. Martha regarded Jesus as a miracle-worker (Jn 11:21-22). When Jesus assured her that her brother would rise again, she took it as commonplace – of course he would rise on the last day! Jesus' response was an 'I am' statement, to indicate what he is in relation to humankind and the world. He declared himself to be the resurrection and the life. One who believes in him will have life beyond death – resurrection life. Indeed, the believer has that life already, and will live fully, forever, beyond death. Martha protested her belief in Jesus – as Messiah, Son of God, the 'one coming into the world'. She had not moved beyond traditional Jewish messianic expectation. Up to now, in the episode, neither Martha nor the disciples have displayed true Johannine faith (vv 17-27).

Martha went to her sister. Her words, 'the Teacher ... is calling for you', recall 10:3, 'he calls his own sheep by name': here was the Good Shepherd (see 20:16). Mary responded to the call; she saw Jesus and knelt at his feet. She acknowledged his presence and displayed unconditional trust in him. She, not Martha, had accepted Jesus as the resurrection and the life. And then, in a peculiar form of Johannine irony, she promptly proceeded to disappoint Jesus.

Verse 33 attests, in this gospel, a startling demonstration of emotion by Jesus. Ostensibly, he wept in bitter grief over the death of a friend. Such human emotion is unexpected in the Johannine Jesus and, in this instance, even more so from a Jesus who knew full well that it was a moment of his 'glorification'. John writes that Jesus was 'greatly disturbed in spirit and deeply moved'. This is strong language. It suggests not conventional grief but bitter disappointment. A Mary who had shown her appreciation of the true nature of Jesus and of what he was about, now joins 'the Jews' (vv 31, 36) in their mourning of the dead and in their estimation of the merely human tears of Jesus. John is precise. Jesus wept (*dakruó*); Mary cried (*klaió*). Jesus was not mourning. He grieved, not over Lazarus (who would be restored to life) but over Mary's 'relapse'.[16] Predictably, 'the Jews' had misunderstood (vv 17-37).

Jesus had been invited to 'come and see' where Lazarus had been buried (v 34). In the event, Jesus was not shown to the tomb; he came to the place. As it will be throughout the passion, already at this approach to 'the hour' Jesus is in charge as he calmly carries through God's purpose. They would 'see the glory of God'. Jesus' prayer was a proclamation to those present that the stupendous event about to take place was deed of the Father. The Father's life-giving power was his as the Sent One. The details of v 44 are deliberately designed to turn the reader's attention to another tomb (19:40-41) and to other grave-clothes (20:5-7). The raising of Lazarus does point to him who is resurrection and life (vv 38-44).

If some of 'the Jews' were prepared to acknowledge Jesus, the 'chief priests and Pharisees' most definitely were not. They agreed that they could not permit him to go on working signs. Sooner or later there would be provocation, and the Romans would surely intervene. They would destroy the temple, and the very nation. Caiaphas, high priest that fateful year, spoke up: 'It is better for you to have

one man die for the people than to have the whole nation
destroyed.' Cynical political opportunism, yes – but much more
than that. Caiaphas was, unawares, making a prophetic pronounce-
ment: Jesus was to die for the salvation of the nation, and of the
world. The death of Jesus would 'gather into one the dispersed
children of God'. One is reminded of 1 Jn 2:2: 'he is the atonement
for our sins, and not for ours only but also for the sins of the whole
world.' Jesus withdrew from the city. He went into the wilderness,
poised for 'the hour' (vv 45-54).

THE HOUR HAS COME (11:55-12:36)

Six days before Passover, Jesus left his wilderness retreat and came
again to Bethany, to the home of Lazarus and his sisters. Martha,
practical hostess, served a meal. The contrast between the women
persists, as In Lk 10:38-42. Mary, the romantic one, took a flask of
expensive ointment and anointed Jesus' feet, and wiped them off
with her long hair. The perfume filled the house, the perfume of
Mary's love. Judas protested the waste. The name of Judas, notoriously familiar to the readers as the betrayer, already signals the
passion of Jesus. An unsavoury factor is the demonisation of Judas,
here 'a thief.' This is in keeping with the gruesome version of the
end of Judas, Mt 27:5; Acts 1:18-19. Instances of the sad human penchant to denigrate, and to trivialise divine mercy.

The Mary who had so disappointed Jesus (11:33) is wholly rehabil-
itated. Now she does respond to the voice of the Good Shepherd
(10:27) and, anticipating the burial of Jesus, she becomes the first to
understand the significance of his death. Many had come from
Jerusalem, not only to meet Jesus, but to see Lazarus, a nine-days
wonder indeed. The chief priests were thinking of doing away with
him also; people were believing in Jesus because of Lazarus (1:55-
12:10).

To Jerusalem (12:12-36)

This visit of Jesus to Jerusalem was unlike his former visits – 2:12-
22; 5:1; 7:10. Here his approach to the city is described as a coming,
not as a 'going up'. He received an enthusiastic reception. A 'great
crowd' met him with cries of 'Hosanna!' and waving branches of

palm. The quotation in v 13 is directly from Ps 118:25-26. The reference is messianic, as in v 15 (see Zech 9:9). The phrase, 'he who comes in the name of the Lord' applies perfectly to Jesus, who comes in the name of and with the power of God.

If there were overtones of nationalistic enthusiasm in the festive welcome, Jesus moved quickly to defuse the situation. 'Jesus found a young donkey and sat on it'; he did not come as a temporal ruler in worldly pomp. Notably, where the text of Zech 9:9 begins 'Rejoice greatly' the Johannine text substitutes, 'Do not fear!' The manner of entry of this humble king anticipates Jesus' declaration to Pilate: 'My kingdom is not from this world' (Jn 18:36). At the time, the disciples were unable to grasp the significance of this messianic entry. Later, after the death of Jesus, they perceived its meaning. The story of the raising of Lazarus was rippling through the enthusiastic crowd. Exasperated Pharisees exclaimed, petulantly: 'We are getting nowhere. Look! the whole world has gone after him!' They spoke more truly than they could ever imagine.

Some God-fearers, Gentiles strongly attracted to Judaism, had come to Jerusalem for Passover. Through Philip (a Greek name) they asked to speak with Jesus. Surprisingly, instead of complying with the request, Jesus stated a fundamental truth to guide all his followers: 'unless a grain of wheat falls into the earth and dies, it remains just a single grain, but if it dies, it bears much fruit' (v 24). Following Christ involves evaluating one's earthly life and possessions, and the readiness to yield everything for his service.

The time for Jesus' passion has come; he fears it, yet longs for it. His soul is troubled. Should he ask the Father to save him from the cross? No! he sets his mind to fulfil his task: 'It is for this reason that I have come to this hour.' Further, he is sure that in this hour of crisis and suffering he will be glorified. Here, in the attitude of Jesus to his coming passion, we find a parallel with Heb 5:7-9. The high priest experiences the pain of obedience, yet accepts it totally, and through it is fulfilled.

Jesus explained more fully in Jn 12:32-33 the relation between his sacrificial death and the life of humankind. The death of Jesus would be his most eloquent sermon: the ultimate revelation of the Father. His death was also judgment on the unbelieving world. It was a death-blow to evil. The 'ruler of this world' is personification of all the opposition of the *archontes*, the 'rulers', to Jesus throughout the ministry and to the cross. His death was firmly positive: 'I, when I am lifted up from the earth, will draw all people to myself.' This lifting-up means, in the language of the fourth gospel, two things. It is both the physical posture of crucifixion (see 3:14, 'as Moses lifted up the serpent in the wilderness ...') and the divine act by which Jesus was glorified, on account of his obedient death. Just as he was lifted up in torment by sinful men (and it was men and not not women who brought about the death of Jesus!), even so was he raised in immortal triumph, by the Father, to be Saviour of all.

'I, when I am lifted up from the earth, will draw all people to myself.' Jesus was doing much more than indicating the manner of his death. The crowd did not catch his meaning. He issued a final warning. He pleaded: Do, do turn to the light. Believe in me while you still have time. I have always spoken in the name of the Father who sent me. The Father is greater than I. Nevertheless, to hear me is to hear the Father, your God. To believe in me is to put your faith in him.

Jesus left them. His mission was ended. Or, was it only beginning? His hour had come (vv 12-36).

The Evangelist's Comment (12:37-50)

The text of Isaiah 6:9-10 is invoked in three New Testament settings: to explain the negative reaction to the parables of Jesus (Mk 4:10-12, parr.), to his 'signs' (Jn 12:37-41) and to Paul's ministry to Jews (Acts 28:25-27). In its Isaian context the declaration of Is 6:9-10 is a forceful and paradoxical proclamation of what, inevitably, is going to happen: the prophet's message will not be heeded. Early Christian thinkers tended to account for the rejection of the message of Jesus by asserting that such, strangely, was will of God. There were always those who did hearken. Some even of the 'authorities' came to believe in Jesus. Like Nicodemus, they remained crypto-disciples. 'They loved human glory more than the glory that comes from God.' The Johannine author is unrelenting in his Two Ways theology (see Deut 30:15-20). He will find scope for dramatic development in the Roman trial of Jesus (vv 37-50).

In vv 44-50 the evangelist has Jesus, who had already left the stage (12:36), cry out his final word. He presents himself as the One Sent. As God's agent, he is the one in whom God is fully present. As agent of this Father he is not in the business of judgment. This Saviour God sent his Son into the world to save the world. Salvation is his one concern. As obedient Son/Agent, Jesus obeys wholly the one who sent him. He obeys a commandment. What a glorious commandment: 'I know that his commandment is eternal life!'

* * *

In the fourth gospel the raising of Lazarus brought the opposition to Jesus to its climax. For Jesus himself it was his final sign. It revealed him as the resurrection and the life. The sisters Martha and Mary illustrate the recurring Johannine theme of coming to faith. Martha did not progress beyond recognition of Jesus as a traditional messianic figure. Mary responded to the call of the Good Shepherd, then wavered, but finally came to full faith by her anointing of Jesus, her recognition of the significance of his death.

Jesus made his messianic entry into Jerusalem, in his own fashion. It was enough to exasperate 'the Jews' – the world had gone after him. The hour had come, the hour of the death of the 'grain of wheat'. Lifted up, he would draw all people to himself.

CHAPTER 6

Meal and Discourse

Apart from me you can do nothing (Jn 15:5)

The hour had come. Before departing, Jesus would tell his disciples, in a manner they could never forget, how utterly he loved them. Jesus knew that he was about to give the supreme manifestation (see 15:13) of his abiding love for his disciples. He himself brought out clearly the meaning of what he did, the act of humble service he now rendered. The opening words (13:1) are a caption for all that is to come in chapters 13-17, the demonstration of Jesus' love for his own – a love to the end (*eis telos*) – without measure: 'Having loved his own who were in the world, he loved them to the end.' Jesus laid aside his garments (13:4,12) as he had spoken of laying down his life (10:18). The disciples were to have 'share' with him (v 8); the washing of the feet expressed symbolically that they are brought into communion of life with Jesus through his death, a supreme act of self-giving and humble service. It is necessary to be washed by Jesus, giver of life, if one is to have part with him in eternal life – one must share in his death and resurrection.

'I have set you an example.' The disciples are not to look only to his ultimate gesture of love; humble service should characterise all the living of his followers. Here is a moving lesson in *diakonia*. Jesus is indeed Lord and Teacher; he has authority. But his style and exercise of authority are marked by service. The whole of Jesus' life, culminating in his death and resurrection, was a passage from 'this world' to the Father, from death to life, for us. 'That you may believe that I AM' (v 19). He had spoken of his betrayal. He cannot mean that the betrayal as such would reveal Jesus as bearer of the divine name and power. He meant that the betrayal would trigger the procedure that would lead to his 'lifting up' and his revelation of himself and the Father (see 8:28). The reality which Christ gives us is himself as the 'man for others'. If we really receive him as such we must ourselves become 'people for others', servants of our fellows. Our challenge is our ongoing 'passage' from selfishness to service (vv 1-20).

Jesus had set an example (v 15). He knew that his example would be ignored. Those who, down the ages, will claim to speak in his name would, too often, speak with arrogant self-assurance. He would, over and over, be betrayed. Jesus' awareness of future betrayals was focused, here and now, on the presence of a traitor at his farewell supper. He declared, 'One of you will betray me.' A favourite disciple, not one of the twelve, who reclined by him, asked who that person was. Jesus told him, quietly, that it was the one to whom he would hand a morsel of bread he had dipped in the common dish. 'When he had dipped the morsel he took it and gave it to Judas' (13:26). Hereby hangs a tale. Some early manuscripts of the gospel omit 'he took it' – it is not in the NRSV, the version I follow; it ought to be! That Jesus took bread occurs in all the gospel feeding stories and in the synoptic and Pauline Last Supper accounts. The phrase, to Christian ears, has unmistakable eucharistic overtones. Francis Moloney's comment is splendidly perceptive:

> Scribes could not tolerate the idea that the sharing of the morsel between Jesus and Judas might have eucharistic overtones and thus they eliminated words that made this association explicit. Just as baptism is a sub-theme to the footwashing, eucharist is a sub-theme to the meal and the gift of the morsel. Within the context of a meal indicated as eucharistic Jesus gives the morsel to the most despised character in the Johannine narrative: Judas. Disciples always have and always will display ignorance, fail Jesus, and deny him. Some may even betray him in an outrageous and public way. But Jesus' never-failing love for such disciples, a love that reached out even to the archetype of the evil disciple, reveals a unique God (cf vv 18-20). This is what it means to love *eis telos* (v 1).[17]

Jesus had assured his own of how wholly he loved them. He would now speak to them his last will and testament. The betrayer had gone to his task. For him 'it was night' (v 30) – he had turned his back on the light of the world. But he had not escaped the care of the shepherd (vv 21-30).

After Judas' departure Jesus was alone with his other disciples. In our text, the general context is that of eucharist which, though never explicitly mentioned, is implicit throughout. 'Now the Son of Man has been glorified.' The 'now' is the hour of decision and consummation, belonging in time, yet decisive for eternity. Now, by going forward to the cross, by being 'lifted up', Jesus is about to achieve his 'glory' – his revelation of his loving Father. Already he had told 'the Jews', 'where I am going you cannot come' (7:34; 8:21-22); but the reason on that occasion was their 'sin'. Here the separation from his disciples is occasioned by his death. While they cannot come to him, he will come to them. In the meantime they will live with his new 'commandment'. The 'newness' here is the newness of the covenant founded and perpetuated in the eucharist. What is new in this covenant is love 'as I have loved you'. Even if Jesus departs and they cannot now follow him to the Father, they can still be 'followers' of Jesus here and now and they can keep his spirit alive among themselves (vv 34-35). As long as they keep true to the 'new commandment', as long as Christian love is in this world (the 'Christian' love, too, of many who do not know him), the world still encounters Jesus.

> An essential idea in the passage vv 31-35 is that when Jesus looks at his death and beyond it, he sees that his human life, far from being a meaningless God-denying absurdity, is instead a place of unprecedented divine generosity and regeneration. It is a place in which God shines forth and in which God's shining reveals Jesus' own true self. God's glorious presence so lights up life that it invites people to love.

> But love is not easy. One cannot love as Jesus has loved, one cannot give oneself as Peter proposes to do, without outside help. There are barricades which make love inaccessible, and so, before speaking of it, before issuing the invitation, Jesus refers to his own going away (v 33), to what is, in fact, a mission to overleap the barricades.

> Through his departure in death he will release a stream of spiritual life which, while sweeping away all obstacles, will impart a new life, a new power of loving.[18]

DEPARTURE (CH 14)

Jesus spoke to console his friends, distressed over his words about going away (13:3-36). They ought not be troubled at a prospect of loneliness. He asks them to 'believe'. Faith in Jesus is faith in God, accepting God for who he really is. His going from them is not abandonment; it is preparation of a home for them. There is ample room for them within the area of communion of life with himself and his Father; there is his Father's house and his own. Communion with Father and Son is his gift to them. He himself is the Way – a way that is the truth and the life. He is the truth who makes known who God really is; he is the life who makes known the one who is source of life. Jesus himself is the way to the ultimate destination, the final abiding with God. This road to God is a sure way because he is the one who leads and takes us to our destination.

Jesus pointed beyond himself: 'Whoever has seen me has seen the Father.' He is revelation of the Father. He is such because he is agent of the Father – the Sent One. He is in the Father and the Father in him because he bears the Father's name and authority. The believer in Son and Father does 'the works of the Father', manifests the oneness of Father and Son. In 1-11 Jesus had described his own closeness to God; in vv 12-14 he went on to indicate how others are brought into a parallel closeness.

This involves a journey: the journey of a believer (v 2) inspired by hope (vv 13-14) and love (vv 15-17). Loving Jesus means listening to his word and putting it into action. To obey is to love. Jesus 'comes' to all who respond in this manner to his love. In response to his asking, the Father will give 'another Paraclete.' The term *paraklétos*, meaning assistant or advocate, occurs only in the Johannine writings. In 1 Jn 2:1 Jesus is a paraclete: 'We have a *paraklétos* with the Father, Jesus Christ the righteous.' Jesus had been a paraclete to his disciples, helping them as their teacher, assisting them in their faith. Now, risen and with the Father (the post-Easter situation is really in view) he will be present to them in another manner. The purpose of 'the Spirit of truth' (the Paraclete), who is 'in' and 'with' the disciples, is to make Jesus present to them. That is why Jesus can go on to promise: 'I will come to you' (v 18). After the death and resurrection of Jesus his Spirit is 'with' the disciples, he dwells 'among' them, he is 'in' them. He is actively present in the awareness of the Johannine community. Through his Spirit-Paraclete presence the message of Jesus had become an effective power in their lives.

Jesus did not leave his disciples orphaned and desolate. Indeed, by their faith, they would be able to 'see' him and share in his life – in the life of Father and Son. Communion with him depends on their response to his word, for only by loving response can they hope to be drawn into that communion of love. We learn that we cannot claim to be one with Jesus Christ, guided by and living according to this Spirit, unless we observe his demands in our everyday lives (vv 15-24).

Jesus continued to speak encouragingly of his departure. Again he referred to the Paraclete. The Father will send the Paraclete as he had sent Jesus because the Paraclete is the continuation of Jesus' presence. Naturally, then, the Paraclete will continue to clarify Jesus' revelation. Jesus conferred the gift of peace – his *shalom,* the fullness of life. His return to the Father should not trouble the disciples. The declaration, 'the Father is greater than I' balances the 'I and the Father are one' of 10:30. Jesus reveals the Father and speaks in his name; that authority has been granted him. Jesus is about to clash, radically, with evil; before him evil is ultimately helpless. As the One Sent he always does as the Father commands. His 'food is to do the will of him who sent him' (4:34). He will do what the Father wants: to make the Father truly known. The time has come to depart: 'Let us be on our way' (v 31). Clearly an original ending. The logical continuation is 18:1. (vv 25-31)

THE TRUE VINE (15:1-16:4a)

The image of the vine recalls the Old Testament designation of Israel as the vine of Yahweh (see Is 15:1-7; Jer 2:21; Ezek 15:1-8; Ps 80:8-19). Jesus declares that he himself, and not the Israel of old, is the real, the genuine, vine of God. From this understanding of the image we may move still further to stress the intimate relationship of branches and stock within the vine. And Jesus does stress the union between him and his disciples. As 'true vine' Jesus is source of real life. The Father remains source of the productivity of the vine.

The Vine (15:1-8)

'I am the vine, you are the branches.' We tend to regard this statement as no more than a figure of speech. Spontaneously, for this is our way of thinking, we take the declaration about the vine to mean that the union of Christ with his own is like the link between the branches and the vine. The disciples are asked to think about a vine, to regard the vital link of branch and trunk. Jesus is thought to say, in effect: the union between us, between you and me, is something like that intimate union in nature. What he means is exactly the opposite! For him the intimate union of vine and branches is a symbol of the infinitely closer union of Jesus with his disciples. That is why Jesus can speak of himself as the genuine vine: the sublime truth which the vine symbolises is fully realised only in him. Understood in this way, the declaration of Jesus is emphatic and clear: we live by the life of the vine; we live by the life of Christ.

Christian life is unthinkable except in terms of Christ. He and the Christian abide one in the other because they share a common life. The branches, however, while living from the sap of the vine, need to be tended. This is the task of the Father. He tends the vine, but its branches will bear fruit only if they are effectively attached to the vine, only if his life flows in them: apart from him they can do nothing, they count for nothing. 'Apart from me you can do nothing', as Jesus can do nothing without the Father (5:19). The Father expects the disciples, his children, to bear fruit. He is glorified – revealed – in the Son, in his obedience and in the perfect accomplishment of his work. It is a short, inevitable step to the glorification – the revelation – of the Father also in the obedience and fruitfulness of those who are joined to the Son. The Father's activity and that of the disciples come together in the production of fruit, with Jesus as the 'vine' and the 'place' where growth and fruit are achieved (vv 1-8).

As I Have Loved You (15:9-11)

The image of the vine has slipped into the background, to reappear, momentarily, in the metaphor of fruit: 'I appointed you to go and bear fruit, fruit that will last' (v 16). The intimate union of vine and branches, which the image had stressed, is now presented as a bond of love which should unite the disciples of Christ. His affection for them is a friendship that knows no limits; he asks that all of them should love one another as friends and bear unmistakably the fruit of charity. To abide in him, to live with his life, is to abide in his love, in the love with which he loves the disciples as the Father had loved him. Jesus had loved his own before he had chosen them; they are to abide in that love which is more his than it is their own.

He went on to show what abiding in his love means. The love of Jesus was modelled on that of the Father. The fidelity of the disciples, in abiding in the divine life and under the divine care, should be modelled on the Son; as he has observed the commandments of his Father, so they should observe his. The parallel shows that love and obedience are mutually dependent: love arises out of obedience, obedience out of love. It follows that authentically Christian obedience can flourish only in an atmosphere of Christian love (vv 9-11).

Love One Another (15:12-17)

The 'commandments' of Jesus may be reduced to one, the commandment of love. Love is the sap of the vine, the bond of existence within the unity of Father, Son and believers. Jesus had hitherto granted to his disciples, to his own, obvious marks of affection and that from the moment he had chosen them (13:1). But now he is going to give them the supreme evidence of his love. Voluntary death, a life freely laid down, will be the characteristic proof of *agapé*, a love which moves out to sacrifice oneself for others. The statement that the greatest love is that which entails the supreme sacrifice is not, however, a definition of love; Jesus means that his sacrifice is the most expressive mark of it. The sense is that nobody can give a more convincing proof of love than one who offers one's life for those whom one loves. And when Jesus adds, 'You are my friends', in effect he is telling them: Nobody has a greater love than that which I have for you. They had not chosen him. He had chosen and called them; he had chosen them to bear fruit. His first and last word: Love one another. They are not only his friends; they are friends one of the other.

Jesus had sketched for his disciples the programme of the Christian apostolate: 'You did not choose me, but I chose you. And I appointed you to go and bear fruit, fruit that will last.' It is he who chooses, calls, and appoints; the initiative is entirely his. The principle of the apostolate is union with Jesus, but the disciples have a task to perform. By bearing the fruit that Jesus expects of them (fruit, even in the apostolate, which may well be hidden from eyes of flesh) they are true children of their heavenly Father. Then they can indeed address him as Abba. Then they can pray to him with absolute confidence.

As for Jesus himself, he does not draft for his disciples an elaborate code of laws. He has no wish to impose a heavy burden on them. He desires to set them free, not to bind them. All that he commands them is reduced to one precept: 'Love one another'. But he is not thereby less demanding. Substitution of the rule of law can effectively stifle further generosity. At any rate, there is no getting away from the fact that the one thing Jesus has asked of us – the one thing that Jesus has commanded us – is to love one another (vv 12-17).

Servants and Master (15:18-16:4a)

Jesus turned to warning that down the road disciples will be treated as he had been treated. They are not greater than their master. They, as he, will be hated by the 'world'. Here *kosmos* has, most emphatically, its hostile Johannine sense: the place of estrangement from God following on the rejection of both Jesus and the Father. The disciples do not belong to this 'world'; they do not live by its standards. The 'world' and discipleship are two clearly separated spheres. Jesus is going to the Father, but they will not be on their own at the mercy of that hostile 'world'. He will 'send' the Paraclete as his 'witness'. The Paraclete will be the invisible but real presence of Jesus when he has gone to be with the Father. Tribulation will not be long in coming. 'They will put you out of the synagogue': this was the experience of the Johannine community. It is 'their hour': reminiscent of Lk 22:53, 'This is your hour, and the power of darkness!' The evangelist is encouraging those of his day discouraged by opposition and persecution (vv 15:18-16:4a).

DEPARTURE (16:4-33)

Role of the Paraclete (16:7-15)

In the farewell discourse we have five passages in which the Paraclete appears, in the latest of them under the synonymous title

'the Spirit of Truth': 14:16-17; 14:25-26; 15:26-27; 16:7-11; 16:13-15.
The Paraclete is the divine power that continues and completes
Jesus' ministry. The Paraclete is the perpetuation of Jesus' presence
among his followers, the presence of Jesus after Jesus had departed.
This emerges clearly in chapter 16: 'I tell you the truth: it is to your
advantage that I go away, for if I do not go away, the Paraclete will
not come to you; but if I go, I will send him to you' (16:7). There is at
least a partial parallel where, earlier, Jesus had told his disciples: 'If
you loved me you would rejoice that I am going to the Father'
(14:28). The departure of Jesus is a paradox. He had assured his disciples. 'I will not leave you orphaned' (14:18). Yet, they must suffer
the loss of him as Jesus if they are to have his abiding presence as
Paraclete, for the Spirit is gift of the glorified Lord and remains
essentially related to Jesus. This point was made in 7:39, 'as yet
there was no Spirit, because Jesus was not yet glorified.' The risen
Jesus gives the Spirit because it is as Paraclete he will henceforth be
present on earth. The statement about Jesus' departure (16:7)
becomes, paradoxically, a promise of his presence, albeit in a different manner. Jesus had already said that the Paraclete would testify
on his behalf (15:26). He had warned that the 'world' that had hated
him would hate his followers (15:18-20). Now we learn that the wit-
ness-bearing Paraclete reflects the conflict state of the church.

'When he comes, he will prove the world wrong about sin and
righteousness and judgment: about sin, because they do not believe
in me; about righteousness, because I am going to the Father and
you will see me no longer; about judgment, because the ruler of this
world has been judged' (16:8-11). This is nothing other than an
anticipation of, and a reversal of, the trial of Jesus. The Paraclete is
witness, and revealer of the truth; he will show the disciples 'where
wrong and right and judgment lie' (NEB). He will prove that the
world is guilty of sin – the basic (Johannine) sin of rejecting the
light, of refusing to accept Jesus. He will prove the world wrong
about righteousness by showing that the Jesus, whom it branded
guilty, is the righteous One. He will demonstrate, with typical
Johannine irony, that in condemning Jesus the world brought judgment on itself. The cross seemed to be the end, the triumph of the
world. In the Paraclete Jesus is still present and the tables have been
turned: 'I, when I have been lifted up from the earth, will draw all

people to myself' (12:32). The hour of passion and death was the moment of naked confrontation of Jesus and evil (12:31; 14:30). Victory over death, the Father's vindication of Jesus, meant that the power of evil had been broken. The Paraclete will not only spell out for the disciples the measure of these events, but his abiding presence with them will be the comforting assurance of the victory of their Lord: 'Take courage: I have conquered the world' (16:33).

In 14:25-26 the Paraclete, who takes Jesus' place, will teach, leading into a fuller understanding of what Jesus had revealed and taught. In 16:13-15 this role of the Paraclete as teacher surfaces again: 'When the Spirit of truth comes, he will guide you into all the truth; for he will not speak on his own, but will speak whatever he hears, and he will declare to you the things that are to come. He will glorify me, because he will take what is mine and declare it to you' (16:13-14). The language is opaque, as not infrequently in John. It is so here because Jesus is speaking obliquely of his future presence. Jesus had told the disciples: 'I still have many things to say to you, but you cannot bear them now' (16:12). Only after his 'glorification' – his full revelation of the Father and of himself – could there be understanding of what was said and done throughout his ministry. After the resurrection the Paraclete will guide them into the full meaning of Jesus and of his teaching. If he will lead them into all the truth, he still will not speak on his own. There is no new revelation because there cannot be new revelation: Jesus is the revelation of the Father, the Word. But what does it mean that he will declare the things that are to come? Rather than an announcement of new revelation, this means a spelling out to successive generations of the contemporary significance of what Jesus had said and done.

In the fourth gospel the Spirit – under the title Paraclete – is the perpetuation of Jesus' presence. The Johannine community was convinced that their Lord abided with them. As Jesus had been 'Teacher and Lord' of his disciples (13:13), so now as Paraclete, he was the sole authority of the community. (In the Johannine writings there is, strikingly, no evidence of any 'ecclesiastical' structure.) John, advisedly, calls the Spirit 'another Paraclete' (14:16) because he is another presence of Jesus. 'As yet there was no Spirit, because Jesus was not yet glorified' (7:39). The evangelist could not have been unaware of the pervasive harking to 'Spirit', the mighty presence of God throughout the Old Testament. He has another 'Spirit' in mind. If, for him, the Spirit can only come when Jesus has departed, it is because his Spirit/Paraclete is presence of that 'absent' Jesus. His continuing presence among his own will no longer be in the figure of the man of Galilee but as life-giving Spirit. As Paraclete, the risen Lord is abidingly present in his church. In this manner the later Christian is assured that she or he is no further removed from the time and ministry of Jesus than the earlier Christian. The Paraclete dwells among us as fully as Jesus 'abode' with his own. See 20:29.

The discourse ends (16:16-33) with words of assurance to the disciples. They had progressed in their understanding of him, but they had not yet grasped the significance of his departure. The 'hour' is, paradoxically, the moment of revelation of the Father (v 25) and moment of flight and abandonment (v 32). In the midst of tribulation they are to be bolstered by prospect of future joy (vv 20-22; see 14:1, 27). They are disciples of a Jesus who is victorious in the darkest moment of abandonment and death (v 33). 'I am not alone because the Father is with me' (v 32). As in Mk 14:50 the disciples may be scattered (Jn 16:32) and Jesus left alone. But never would the Johannine Jesus cry out: 'My God, my God, why have you forsaken me?' (Mk 15:34; see Jn 12:27-28). The closing word of Jesus is a resounding word of encouragement: 'In the world you face persecution. But take courage; I have conquered the world!' A Johannine disciple had heard this word: 'This is the victory that conquers the world, our faith. Who is the one who conquers the world but the one who believes that Jesus is the Son of God?' (1 Jn 5:4-5).

JESUS CLOSING PRAYER (CH 17)

The farewell discourse closes with a prayer. This prayer is, in its manner, a commentary on the passion of Jesus which reflects the drift of the fourth gospel's emphasis: the coming of Jesus, revealer of the Father, into this world (17:1-12), then the return of Jesus to the Father. Structurally, the prayer falls into three parts as Jesus prays for himself (vv 1-5), for his disciples (vv 6-19) and for the community of the future who 'believe through their word' (vv 20-26).

For Himself (17:1-5)

'The hour has come', the hour of death-and-resurrection. It is the hour of the glory of Jesus, 'glory' being the revelation of God in power. Only in death-and-resurrection does Jesus fully reveal himself and reveal the Father. And only by laying down his life for his friends, out of love, is Jesus able to give the lifegiving Spirit (7:39). 'Glorify the Son': the 'glorifying' of the Son necessarily involves the glorifying of the Father – making the Father known because the self-disclosure of Jesus is geared to the revelation of the unseen God.

If the Son has been given power over 'all flesh' – all humankind – it is that he may bestow 'eternal life'. Eternal life is 'knowledge': to leave oneself free to receive eternal life one must know, one must have experienced, the loving relationship of Father and Son. Here, 'to know', as in the Old Testament, means to have communion with God. A revealing parallel is 1 Jn 1:3: 'our fellowship is with the Father and with his Son Jesus Christ' where 'fellowship' (*koinónia*) is the same as 'to know' in our text. Jesus' whole concern had been to make the Father known. Yet, the 'hour' of his death and resurrection is the high moment of that revelation. So Jesus prays to the Father.

For His Disciples (17:6-19)

In vv 6-19 Jesus prays for his disciples. He prays for those present at the meal (ch 13) – he had taken care to make the Father known to them. Indeed, they were the Father's gift to him in the first place. They know that the Father is source of all that Jesus had done for them. Jesus had given them 'the words' of the Father – he had revealed the Father. Jesus had come into the world because God so loved the world that he gave his only Son (3:16) in order to save the world of humankind (3:17). Jesus, who is now sending his disciples into the world, to speak again his word of salvation, cannot pray for that hostile world. The disciples are being sent, as Jesus was sent, to challenge the world, so that people might at last turn from darkness to light. He prays for those whom he leaves behind to carry on his work. He commits them to the Father's care and prays especially that they may experience among themselves the warm communion of Father and Son.

Though regularly unperceived, v 12 raises a basic issue: the whole question of divine mercy and forgiveness. 'I guarded them, and not one of them was lost except the one destined to be lost' (17:12). This (NRSV) rendering reflects the current verdict, traditionally and of scholars, that Judas is envisaged. It is essential to decide how one understands the expression *ho huios tés apóleias*. Rendered by NRSV as 'the one destined to be lost' it is, literally, 'the son of perdition.' (NRSV, margin, 'the son of destruction'.) The expression occurs again only in 2 Thess 2:3, 8-9, where it refers to a Satanic figure. John, then, is referring to Satan, not to Judas.

> 'Often regarded as a reference to Judas, this expression must be given the meaning it has in the only other place it appears in the NT: Satan (2 Thess 2:3, 8-9). The only person in the story Jesus could not "care for" is Satan who planned the betrayal (cf 13:2). Jesus washed the feet and shared the morsel with Judas despite Satan's designs (cf 13:2) ... Jesus has kept and cared for all the disciples entrusted to him by the Father, including Judas. As his gestures in 13:1-17, 21-38 indicate, not even Judas can be judged as lost.'[19]

One makes an issue of this because of a concern with a perennial human penchant to trivialise the wondrous mercy and forgiveness of God. Jesus was well aware of this (see Lk 15:1-32; Mt 18:23-35). This attitude finds unsavoury expression in the demonisation of Judas. In Jn 12:6 he had become a petty thief. It was assumed that he had to have come to a sticky end – hence two, wholly contradictory, versions of his death: Mt 27:3-10; Acts 1:18-20. We should learn that we are better advised to leave not only others, but ourselves in the hands of a merciful, forgiving and infinitely loving God – the God whose love reached the limit: he did not spare his own Son.

Verse 13 opens the theme of Jesus' return to the Father. He speaks, while he is still with them, so that the disciples he is leaving behind may find the joy which follows on the fulfilment of the command-ment of love. In bearing witness before the world they must, as he, suffer the world's hate. But that is a feature of their task, as it was of his. The Father will 'protect them from the evil one' – surely an echo of the Lord's Prayer (Mt 6:13). The disciples will be consecrated in the truth, that is to say, in God's word – the truth that is Jesus' revel-ation of the unseen God. To be consecrated in the truth means to have a closer union with Jesus who is Truth (14:6). They have accepted him and kept his word (17:6-14); now they must bring him and his words to others. Jesus sends them as he himself was sent; the mission of his community of faith is to continue the mission of Jesus. By his death (his 'sanctification') Jesus will confirm and consecrate his disciples. His death is a sacrifice: the supreme priestly action on their behalf (vv 16-19).

For the Community (17:20-26)

The mission of the disciples (vv 6-19) will be efficacious, made so by the prayer of Jesus. The power of his prayer reaches out to those others, those who will come to 'believe in him'; for faith means a personal relationship with Jesus, union with him. And Jesus prays that the community be one. Unity follows on the communion of Christians with Father and Son. The missionary role is not lost to sight: 'that the world may believe'. Those later disciples, like the initial group, are sent, as the Master was, 'to testify to the truth' (18:37). 'Glory' will be theirs as, in their turn and measure, they make Father and Son known. But they can have this 'glory,' this revealing role, only if they are one with Father and Son and with one another. Only so will they be witness to a God who is love.

If Jesus had prayed that his disciples should be taken out of the world (17:15) that was in view of their task of carrying on his work. As he had come into the world to do the saving will of the Father and, the task accomplished (19:30), to return in glory to that beloved Father, so he wills and prays that his disciples, when they have accomplished their task, will enjoy unending blessedness with him. Then, for them too, the message that they had preached will be wholly clear. They will see, and share in, the perfect union of Father and Son and glow in their love. All will be achieved in and through their being with Jesus, fully and forever. It is because the Father had given them to the Son, and because they had been joined with him on earth, as branches of the vine, that they will be united with him forever. They are those who have known Father and Son, and that is what eternal life is all about (17:3).

The closing words of the prayer bring us back to earth. Jesus will make the Father more deeply known. But that will be at the cost of love. It is only as a loving community that the love of Father and

Son can be experienced, that Father and Son can be truly known. Only in loving one another can the disciples be one with Jesus; only so will he dwell among them and be in them. It is the earnest prayer of Jesus that this be so: 'I pray for them' (17:20).

* * *

As the hour approached, Jesus was set on assuring his disciples how utterly he loved them. His washing of their feet was a moving gesture. It was also a challenge to them. He was faithful to all of his own.

He spoke at length to console his friends, saddened at his speaking of departure. He will not leave them orphaned: he will come, as Paraclete, to abide with them. They must remember that they are branches of him, the vine – branches that should bear fruit – and realise that without him they are helpless. They are not his servants; they are his friends. They will be deprived of him for a little while. He will see them again and they will rejoice. And they will have the assurance that he had conquered the world.

In his closing solemn prayer, Jesus prayed for himself, for the consolation of his disciples, and for all down the ages who, fruit-bearing branches of the vine, would continue his task.

CHAPTER 7

Death and Life

He bowed his head and gave up his Spirit (Jn 19:30)

The Arrest (18:1-11)

When Jesus had ended the solemn prayer of ch 17 he went, with his disciples, across the Kidron valley to a garden. Judas, who knew the place, guided a Roman military attachment and some temple police. Jesus, fully aware of all that was to happen, took the initiative and strode forward to accost the band. They declared that they sought 'Jesus of Nazareth'. At the God-presence in him, manifest in his affirmation 'I am' *(egó eimi)* they were rendered powerless, stricken to the ground. Jesus, completely in charge of the situation, laid down his terms: they may arrest him, on condition that they did not detain his disciples. Judas is included among those who must be permitted to go free. 'I did not lose a single one of those whom you gave me' (v 9): a paraphrase of the assurances of 6:39; 17:12. Judas, too, had been given by the Father and he stands within the Father's loving care. Simon Peter struck out impetuously and cut off the right ear of Malchus; he was rebuked by Jesus. Only now was Jesus arrested, and only because he permitted it.

The Passion (18:12-19:42)

John presents the passion as the triumph of the Son of God. The *dramatis personae* are sharply characterised. Despite appearances, Jesus is always in control. He is the Judge who judges his judge (Pilate) and his accusers ('the Jews'). He is the King who reigns, with the cross for a throne: 'I, when I am lifted up from the earth, will draw all to myself.' The Jews are not the whole Jewish people but its leaders who see Jesus as a danger to them, the establishment, and who are determined to destroy him.

Such are 'the Jews' in the story-line. For John and his contemporaries 'the Jews' are the leaders of a later Judaism vigorously opposed to the now distinctive Christian movement. Pilate recognises, and three times acknowledges, the innocence of Jesus. He desperately tries to compromise but ends by yielding to political blackmail. He is a man who will not make a decision for or against Jesus – and finds himself trapped.

Jesus Before the Jewish Authorities (18:12-24)

Jesus was brought before Annas, a former high priest who had been deposed by the Romans but who still had considerable influence. This was not a formal trial but an interrogation. Jesus was questioned about his disciples and his teaching. His answer was that he had taught 'plainly', in face of 'the world'. He implies that the word is still available through his disciples. The episode throws light on the confrontation of the evangelist and his community with contemporary Judaism. Jesus becomes a defender of his followers against attacks of Judaism. Jesus was then sent to Caiaphas the actual high priest. In view of his earlier cynical political decision (and unwitting prophecy), 'it is better for you to have one man die for the people' (11:50), Jesus cannot expect justice. As in the synoptics John, too, has Peter's denials of Jesus (18:15-18, 25-27).

Jesus Before Pilate (18:28-19:16a)

The synoptic accounts of the trial before Pilate tell us little, whereas John's dramatic reconstruction does bring out the significance of it. Only John makes clear why Jesus was brought to Pilate in the first place and why Pilate gave in to having him crucified. Only John shows the interplay of subtle (and not so subtle) political forces on Pilate and indicates how Pilate's original questioning of Jesus concerned a political charge against him. Yet Mark, we now realise, has given the key to the trial in the title 'King of the Jews' (15:2); thereafter he stresses that it is as King of the Jews (Messiah) that Jesus is rejected by the crowd and crucified. In John this theme of Jesus' royal status dominates the encounter between Pilate and Jesus. Recognition or rejection of it is the decisive issue for Pilate and 'the Jews'. It is they who are on trial.

There is a further theological reason for John's stress on the Roman trial. We are to see Pilate in the light of the rest of the fourth gospel. He provides an example of an attitude to Jesus which purports to be neither faith nor rejection: the typical attitude of those who try to maintain a middle position in an all or nothing situation. Pilate's reluctance to make a decision for or against the Light leads to disaster. Because Pilate will not face the challenge of deciding for the Truth in Jesus and against the Jews, he thinks he can persuade the Jews to accept a solution that will make it unnecessary for him to declare for Jesus. This is the Johannine view of the episodes of Barabbas, the scourging, and the delivery of Jesus to the Jews as 'your King'. For John, this trial is our own tragic history of temporising and indecision. Pilate, the would-be neutral man, is frustrated by the pressure of others. He failed to listen to the truth and decide in its favour. He, and all who would follow him, inevitably end up enslaved to this world.

The Johannine presentation of the Roman trial is highly dramatic.[20] It is structured in seven episodes or scenes. There are two settings or stages: the outside court of the praetorium where 'the Jews' are gathered; the inside room where Jesus is held prisoner. Pilate moves back and forth from one stage to the other. The atmosphere is notably different in either setting. Inside, Jesus and Pilate engage in calm dialogue; outside is clamour as Pilate is pressurised to find Jesus guilty. Pilate's passing from one setting to the other is expressive of an internal struggle: while becoming increasingly convinced of Jesus' innocence he finds himself being forced to condemn him.

SCENE 1: OUTSIDE

Jews Demand Death (18:28b-32)

The Jews who had brought Jesus to Pilate would not enter the Gentile praetorium. To do so would involve ritual defilement and prevent them from celebrating Passover. Pilate went out to them; they insisted that Jesus was a criminal deserving death. The execution would be according to Roman law: death by crucifixion. Jesus had already referred to his death as a 'lifting up' – on a cross! 'And I, when I am lifted up from the earth, will draw all people to myself' (12:32).

SCENE 2: INSIDE

Jesus and Pilate on Kingship (18:33-38a)

Pilate questioned Jesus: 'Are you the King of the Jews?' Jesus wanted to know how he understood the title: in a political or in a religious sense? He himself proclaimed the otherworldly realm of truth; he separated his kingship from anything that could threaten Pilate. His purpose was to bear witness to 'the way things really are' – the way God is, the way God is related to the world. 'What is truth?' – Pilate rejected Jesus' offer. He does not belong to God.

SCENE 3: OUTSIDE

Pilate finds Jesus not guilty (18:38b-40)

Pilate had shown that he was not on the side of truth. He had turned from the light. He was the one on trial. He went outside and declared that, having interrogated Jesus, he could find no case against him. Verse 38a is the first of Pilate's three 'not guilty' statements (see 19:4, 6). He tried the ploy of the Passover amnesty: 'Do you want me to release for you the King of the Jews?' They shouted back: 'We want Barabbas' – a known bandit.

SCENE 4: INSIDE

Soldiers Scourge Jesus (19:1-3)

Pilate, in failing to grant Jesus justice, is forced to a travesty of justice. He ordered Jesus to be scourged. Scourged though he had already pronounced him innocent! His scourging of an innocent man proves that man's innocence! Pilate is getting more deeply embroiled. The soldiers twisted some thorn branches into a mock crown (diadem) and decked Jesus in a castoff soldier's cloak. They saluted him: 'Hail, King of the Jews!' The kingship theme, already introduced in the dialogue with Pilate, would persist. Ironically, this mockery serves as a declaration of who Jesus is. John strengthens the kingship motif. In the synoptic narrative, Jesus was stripped of his 'regal' trappings (see Mk 15:20); in John Jesus goes to the cross dressed as a king.

SCENE 5: OUTSIDE

'Behold the Man!' (19:4-8)

Pilate had Jesus presented to the crowd – all bloody as he was from the scourging and decked in the mock crown and robes: 'Here is the

man!' He was showing them a pathetic human being who was no
threat to either Rome or 'the Jews'. Pilate declared, 'I am bringing
him out to you,' but, 'Jesus came out': he is still master of his destiny. It is an ironical presentation of Jesus as the Son of Man. The
crowd howled for his death: 'Crucify him!' In exasperation Pilate
retorted: 'Crucify him yourselves; I have no case against the man.'
They shot back: 'According to our Law he ought to be put to death:
he has claimed to be Son of God.' Here is the theological reason
why 'the Jews' brought Jesus to trial before Pilate. This claim was
emerging as the great issue between Jesus and Christians – viewed
by the former as a threat to monotheism.

SCENE 6: INSIDE

Pilate and Jesus on Power (19:9-11)

Pilate was now quite alarmed: the unbelieving politician is super-
stitious. He came inside and asked Jesus: 'Where are you from?'; it
is the fundamental question of Johannine christology. Jesus was
silent. When Pilate invoked his authority he was told bluntly: 'You
would have no authority over me if it had not been decreed so from
above; but those who have handed me over to you are more guilty
than you.' Jesus' ultimate authority is 'from above'. Pilate was now
desperately anxious to release Jesus. He had been challenged by
Truth – and had sought to compromise. He was hopelessly trapped.
His next attempt to have the case dismissed was met with naked
blackmail: 'If you set this man free you are not Caesar's friend; anyone who makes himself king is a challenge to Caesar.' Pilate was
aware that his standing in Rome was, just then, not very secure; he
could not risk a suggestion of disloyalty to the emperor. Time had
run out on him. He could no longer evade a decision.

SCENE 7: OUTSIDE

The Jews Obtain Death (19:12-16a)

Pilate yielded to the Jewish demand for Jesus' crucifixion. John's
account of the passing of the sentence of death is detailed, dramatic
and theological; the only points of parallel with the synoptics are in
the repeated call for crucifixion and the outcome of Jesus' being
'handed over'. The Old Testament background to this verb (*para-
didómi*), used by all the evangelists, implies that Jesus was 'delivered

up' to his enemies 'according to the definite plan and foreknowl-
edge of God' (Acts 2:23); there was a mysterious divine purpose.
The real trial was over when 'the Jews' uttered the fateful words:
'We have no king but Caesar.' This is akin to the statement in
Matthew's account: 'His blood be on us and on our children!' (Mt
27:25). Both evangelists are reflecting not history but apologetic theology. The tragedy of Jesus' death was viewed through the hostility
between church and synagogue in the late first century AD. The
audience at the trial is made to voice a Christian interpretation of
the Jewish rejection of Jesus.

John also tells us that this was the hour when the Passover lambs
were being sacrificed in the temple. It is supreme Johannine irony:
the Jews renounce the covenant at the very moment when the
priests begin to prepare for the feast which annually recalled God's
deliverance of his covenanted people. By the blood of a lamb in
Egypt Yahweh had marked them off to be spared as his own. Now,
they know no king but the emperor and they slay another lamb. At
that moment, just before the Passover, as Jesus set out for Golgotha
to shed his saving blood, the trial of Jesus ends with the fulfilment
of that proclamation at the start of the gospel: 'Here is the lamb of
God who takes away the sin of the world!' (1:29).

The Crucifixion of Jesus (19:16b-27)

Jesus was led out, laden with the cross-beam and without human
assistance, to Golgotha, the Place of the Skull. 'Carrying the cross by
himself' – there is no Simon of Cyrene: John's christology has no
room for Jesus' needing or accepting help. Jesus was crucified
between two others. Pilate had ordered an inscription which was
affixed to the cross: 'Jesus of Nazareth, the King of the Jews'; he had
the notice written in Hebrew, Latin and Greek. The annoyed Jews
protested: 'It should read, "this man claims to be king of the Jews".'
Pilate retorted: 'What I have written, I have written.' As representative of imperial Rome Pilate had made a heraldic proclamation,
couched in the sacred and secular languages of the day – a world-
wide proclamation of Jesus' Kingship. Supreme irony! This King is
drawing all people to himself (12:32).

In 19:25-27 John has by the cross the Mother of Jesus and the
Beloved Disciple. The mother of Jesus was the first person in the

story to trust unconditionally in the word of Jesus (2:3-5). Now, lifted up on the cross, Jesus bids her accept the Beloved Disciple as her son. He bids that model disciple accept the mother of Jesus as his mother. Jesus had established a new family. 'Because of the cross and from the moment of the cross a new family of Jesus has been created. The Mother of Jesus, a model of faith, and the disciple whom Jesus loved and held close to himself are one as the disciple accepts the Mother in an unconditioned acceptance of the word of Jesus.'[21]

The scene is surely symbolic as a new relationship is set up between the mother and the disciple. The disciple 'took her to his own'. The model disciple obeys unquestioningly the word of Jesus. Mark tells us that, at the crucifixion, 'there were also women looking on from a distance' (Mk 15:40; see Mt 27:55; Lk 23:49) and makes no mention of the mother or of any male disciple. It is wholly unlikely that women and a follower of the condemned Jesus would have been permitted to stand at the very place of execution. Here the theological creativity of John is very much in evidence.

Jesus' Last Words (19:28-30)

Jesus was conscious that his hour had drawn to its close; all had now been accomplished. In response to his call, 'I thirst,' John notes that a sponge full of sour wine was raised to his lips 'on a branch of hyssop' – a small plant that could not sustain a sponge. Pointedly, in Ex 12:22 it is specified that hyssop be used to sprinkle the blood of the Passover lamb on the doorposts of the Israelite homes. Plausibly, John introduced the unlikely hyssop here to suggest that Jesus was fulfilling the role of the Passover lamb. The last word of Jesus, 'It is finished!' is a cry of victory: now Jesus will draw all people to himself. 'Then he bowed his head and handed over the Spirit' (v 30b). In 7:37-39 Jesus promised that when he was glorified those who believed in him would receive the Spirit. His last breath was the outpouring of the life-giving Spirit – his Spirit.

Aftermath of the Death (19:31-37)

The final details, the not breaking of Jesus' legs and the flow of blood and water, have no parallel in the synoptics. True Passover

Lamb, not one bone of Jesus was broken (see Ex 12:46). The flow of blood and water is another proleptic reference to the giving of the Spirit, following on Jn 19:30. There is more to it. Remarkable is v 35, the narrator's insistent testimony to that flow of blood and water. It is surely a word to the reader. The 'water' of baptism (see 3:5) and the 'blood' of the eucharist (see 6:34, 54, 55-56) are here linked with the cross. Jesus, physically absent from the community, is, nonetheless, present in Spirit (19:30), baptism and eucharist. The Johannine communtiy is urged 'to believe' this, to take it to heart. Note that blood and water flow from the dead Jesus. The drama of the cross does not end in death but in the flow of life that comes from death. The death of Jesus on the cross is the beginning of Christian life.

The Burial of Jesus (19:38-42)

Joseph of Arimathea, a recent disciple of Jesus, got permission from Pilate to remove the body of Jesus. He and that other secret disciple, Nicodemus, now 'came out' and gave Jesus a royal burial. They bound his body in linen cloths, sprinkling a lavish quantity of perfumed spices between the folds. Then they laid him in a new unused tomb in a nearby garden. The whole is historically quite at odds with the 'dishonourable burial' account in Mk 15:42-47.

Previously in John's gospel, believers who adhered to Jesus and were identified as his disciples have been contrasted with those who believed but were afraid to have it known that they were disciples. At this 'hour' of the death and burial of Jesus the beloved disciple in 19:31-37 is the example *par excellence* of the first group of believers. Hitherto Joseph and Nicodemus in 19:38-42 have belonged to the second group; but now they are presented as transformed through Jesus' victory on the cross.[23]

THE RESURRECTION (20:1-29)

John has preserved two versions of what, in the synoptic tradition, is the womens' visit to the tomb, Jn 20:1-3 and 11-13. Underlying the first of them (vv 1-2) would seem to be the earliest form of an empty tomb narrative in any gospel. John has introduced the Beloved Disciple and has, for his own dramatic purpose, reduced the original group of women to Mary Magdalene, preparing the way for the later Christophany to her (vv 14-18). It is this christophany, and not an angelic spokesman, which explains the meaning of the empty tomb (vv 12-13). But the tradition which was thus rewritten is very early indeed. In vv 1-2 Mary Magdalene is not a believer but one quite confused.

Thoroughly Johannine is 20:1-10. At Mary Magdalene's disturbing news (v 2) 'Peter and the other disciple' hurried to the tomb. In the tradition, Peter's companion was unnamed. John has introduced him as the Beloved Disciple so that his coming to faith might interpret the significance of the empty tomb. The burial cloths and, more unexpectedly, their arrangement, are a sign that Mary's interpretation of the empty tomb ('they have taken the Lord out of the tomb,' 20:2) is not the correct one. Jesus had not been 'taken' anywhere. Rather, he had left mortality behind him. Only the Beloved Disciple (vv 2, 8) seeing the sign, believed – 'he saw and believed' (v 8). Manifestly, he believed, even before any appearance of the risen Lord, in the risen Christ himself. The fact of the matter is that while the 'beloved disciple' is a real person and the source of John's tradition, he also represents the Christian disciple who is sensitive, in faith and love, to the presence of the risen Jesus. With this one exception – theological exception – of the Beloved Disciple who saw with eyes of faith, the 'empty tomb' is never regarded as a reason for faith. The conviction that Jesus can no longer be found in the tomb because he is risen Lord (and not for any other reason) follows on encounter with the risen Lord.

What is the significance of the resurrection of Jesus? The confession, 'God raised Jesus from the dead', implies more, much more, than the deed of raising from death. It implies that the kingdom of God – the rule of God – has indeed come in Jesus. The resurrection should not be regarded in isolation. In declaring, 'Christ is risen' one is acknowledging that God's saving promises have been accomplished in Jesus. Jesus had seen his whole life and his whole mission in relation to the fulfilment of such promises: 'We had hoped that he was the one to redeem Israel' (Lk 24:21). It was because of their former hope in him that the disciples were able to interpret the resurrection as God's confirmation of all that Jesus stood for. Because he was raised from the dead, Jesus holds decisive significance for us. Because of the fact of his resurrection we know that meaningless death – and meaningless life – now have meaning. Jesus died with the cry on his lips: 'My God, my God, why have you forsaken me?' (Mk 15:34). The sequel was to show that God had never abandoned Jesus. We have the assurance that he will not abandon us. We do, for our comfort, need Marcan christology to balance the Johannine.

Jesus Appears to Mary Magdalene (20:11-18)

Mary, at the tomb (vv 11-13), has not advanced beyond the confusion of vv 1-2. Quite like Luke's Emmaus story where the two disciples conversed with the 'stranger' (Lk 24:13-19), Mary speaks with this 'stranger' (Jn 20:14-15). She recognised him at his calling her by name. This reminds us of 10:3 – the Good Shepherd 'calls his own sheep by name'. Her joyous instinct was to cling to him. She has to learn that the time of association with the earthly Jesus is past. His 'hour' is still in process – the 'hour' of death, resurrection and return to the Father. Mary is given a mission: apostle to the disciples. She brings an astounding message. Up to now, in the narrative, Jesus alone was Son. Now, he speaks of my Father and your Father, my God and your God! The God and Father of Jesus is God and Father of his 'brethren'. Christians are no longer Jesus' disciples, not even his 'friends' (15:15), but his brothers and sisters. Mary Magdalene went – a journey that was a journey of faith. 'I have seen the Lord'; she, also, had achieved the fullness of Johannine faith. 'Another foundational character from the earliest Christian community has journeyed from the darkness of unfaith through a partial faith into perfect belief.'[22]

In the House (20:19-29)

Though the disciples had been assured by Mary Magdalene that the Lord was risen, they hide away 'for fear of the Jews'; the message of the good news does not spare Christians from fear. Jesus came to dispel their fear and bring the peace that only he can grant. At his death Jesus had breathed his Spirit on that little family at the foot of the cross. Now he breathes the Spirit upon this community.

It is significant that in John the church is founded by the risen Lord. When Jesus breathed upon the disciples a new creation was taking place. Just as God made 'the man' into a living being by breathing life into him (Gen 2:7), and as in Ezekiel 37 the dead bones of Israel were stirred to life by the breath of God, so the life of the church comes from the breath of the Spirit of Jesus. This is the new, eternal life, which Jesus brings to being, which plays such a major part in John's gospel. In this sense, everything is already accomplished when Jesus breathes life into his disciples. And he entrusts them with a mission. The mission is nothing more or less than the one he had received from the Father and, indeed, accomplished by his death and resurrection: the reconciliation of men and women with their Parent (the forgiveness of sin). To carry out their mission they are enlivened and inspired by the Holy Spirit, which is Christ's Spirit, making them one with him. They are to be Christ to the world. They will be channels of God's forgiveness of sin and will lay bare sinfulness.

The episode of Thomas (vv 24-29) is of great importance for the fourth evangelist and is, indeed, climactic in his gospel. The disciple, Thomas, passed from unbelief to belief. Thomas had refused to accept the word of the other disciples and insisted on having personal proof of the reality of the resurrection of Jesus (vv 24-25). In the event, he came to belief without need of the crude verification he seemed to demand (20:25, 27-28). It was enough to have seen (v 29). Nonetheless, v 27 is the assurance that the risen Jesus is the crucified Jesus. It is unfortunate that Thomas has been remembered for his stubbornness – 'doubting Thomas.' He deserves to be remembered for the most forthright confession of faith in the gospel: 'My Lord and my God.' The text should be interpreted in the same way as similar texts in chapter 12 ('Whoever sees me sees the Father' and 'the Father and I are one'). As the One Sent Jesus is, at a very deep level, one with the Father. Today we might say that Jesus is wholly transparent to God. Thomas' confession is an acknowledgment and proclamation of the God revealed in Jesus. It is, likely, a confessional formula of the evangelist's church.

Thomas has made the last utterance of a disciple of Jesus. The evangelist adds a comment that is crucial for all disciples of the risen Lord. 'Have you believed because you have seen me? Blessed are those who have not seen and yet have come to believe'(v 29). The evangelist is writing for a generation that has not 'seen' the Lord, for whom Jesus is absent. Here is a word of consolation. This later generation of believers is not less privileged than the foundational disciples. They share with them a common faith in the Lord, though

he be not visible. In a sense, they are more blessed; they have
believed without seeing. We recall that the Beloved Disciple had
already believed without seeing (20:8). These Johannine Christians
are his true disciples.

THE CONCLUSION OF THE GOSPEL (20:30-31)

Christians who have not seen and yet believed have been declared
blessed (30:29). Now, in this conclusion, they are told that all that
has gone before, in this gospel, has been written for them. In the
story, disciples, again and again, were summoned from unfaith,
through partial faith into authentic faith. The readers are presumed
to have attained genuine faith. They are now being urged to persist
in their faith and to deepen it: 'But these are written so that you may
go on believing ...'. They are to believe, wholly, that Jesus is
Messiah, a Messiah who is Son of God. He is the 'one sent' who has
made the Father fully known. As such, he is giver of eternal life.
They will have this life in virtue of their believing relationship with
him.

* * *

It is the desire of the author that all those who read this book or
hear its proclamation be a community of beloved disciples. The
book was written so that a narrative that reports *how* Jesus had
lived his story might confirm *what* was proclaimed in the
Prologue. The author believes passionately that Jesus' life story
proves the claims made for him in the Prologue.[23]

The conclusion to the fourth gospel, which states the purpose of the
gospel, does also state the purpose of all the gospels. All of them are
concerned with christology and discipleship. They are written to
deepen understanding of Jesus so that deeper knowledge of him
and faith in him will inspire and lead to a richer life of discipleship.

Conclusion (21:1-25)

The gospel proper has ended at 20:30-31; this chapter 21 is an appendix. After an introductory listing of the disciples concerned (vv 1-3), we have an appearance of Jesus by the lakeside, Peter's reaction, and the miraculous draught of fish (vv 4-8); then Peter's hauling the net ashore, followed by breakfast with Jesus (vv 9-14); and finally the commissioning of Peter and the prophecy of his death (vv 15-19). The chapter is built around Peter and the Beloved Disciple. In a fishing scene and at a meal Jesus reveals himself to his disciples; he invites them to faith. The ease and intimacy of his meeting with them is reminiscent of their first meeting (1:37-39). But the disciples have difficulty in recognising him (21:4,12). This is a constant feature of the resurrection narratives in all gospels: the Lord is not at once recognised; it required some word or familiar gesture to make him known. This is an effective way of making the point that Jesus had not returned to life as before but had passed, beyond death, to new life with God. He is Jesus – and yet he is different – transformed. Though Peter will be given the more important role (vv 7, 11) it is the Beloved Disciple who is sensitive in faith to the presence of the risen Jesus and recognised him (v 7).

The miraculous catch of fish, with its symbolic reference to 'fishers of people' (Lk 5:10), is summons to an apostolic mission. At the lakeside breakfast Jesus 'took the bread and gave it to them' (v 13). His gesture answers the question how Jesus remains present to his disciples: he is present among them as they share the eucharistic meal.

In vv 15-19 Peter, who had failed his Master (18:15-27), is now reinstated and is entrusted with a pastoral mission. Peter's story is one of calling, falling and recalling. It is noteworthy that he is entrusted with 'my lambs and my sheep'. The Lord is, and remains,

95

'the chief Shepherd' (1 Pet 5:4); there can be no other. Peter asks of
the Beloved Disciple: 'Lord, what about him?' (v 22). The actual situation is that both Peter and the Beloved Disciple are dead and the
Johannine community is coming to terms with a new and difficult
situation. It has linked up with the Great Church but continues to
extol its revered founder. It is he, that Beloved Disciple, who is
source of their distinctive story of the life and teaching, death and
resurrection of Jesus. He is an anonymous saint – and they are the
best kind! Verse 25, as conclusion of the epilogue, is a conscious
echo of the original conclusion (20:30-31). The fourth gospel is,
indeed, *a* story of Jesus. It is not the whole story.

* * *

Jesus was arrested, but on his terms. He took command and was in
command to the end. He spoke forthrightly to the high priest. The
trial before Pilate is high drama as Jesus and Pilate dialogued. It
became increasingly clear that Pilate was the one on trial. At the
end, after thrice pronouncing Jesus not guilty, he condemned an
innocent man.

Carrying his own cross, Jesus went to Golgotha. In a closing gesture
he confirmed the Mother and Beloved Disciple as models of faith.
Jesus chose his moment of death – the moment when all is fulfilled.
His last breath was bestowal of the Spirit. As Passover Lamb, not a
bone of him was broken. He was given a royal burial by two erst-
while hidden disciples.

The Beloved Disciple was the one who understood the meaning of
the empty tomb. Mary Magdalene recognised the voice of the Good
Shepherd. She was sent (*apostolos*) to proclaim the good news. Jesus
came to his disciples to bestow on them the Spirit – his new presence. Thomas became the occasion of our comfort: the blessedness
of those who believe without seeing. This gospel, like each gospel,
was concerned throughout with christology and discipleship.

An Epilogue narrates the rehabilitation of Peter and confirms the
status of the Beloved Disciple. Both are dead. The Good News
abides.

Notes

1. Harrington, Wilfrid J., *Mark: Realistic Theologian. The Jesus of Mark; Luke: Gracious Theologian. The Jesus of Luke; Matthew: Sage Theologian. The Jesus of Matthew*, (Dublin: The Columba Press, 1996, 1997, 1998).
2. Moloney, Francis J., *The Gospel of John.*, Sacra Pagina 4. A Michael Glazier Book (Collegeville, MN: The Liturgical Press, 1998).
3. Harrington, Wilfrid J., *Mark: Realistic Theologian*, 8-10.
4. Hanson, Anthony J., *The Prophetic Gospel* (Edinburgh: T. & T. Clark, 1991), 32.
5. Moloney, F. J., *op. cit.*, 41.
6. Harrington, W. J., *op. cit.*, 24-27.
7. This is the first instance of a recurring pattern. Again and again Jesus is inadequately estimated until, at the climax, he is recognised and acknowledged for who he really is. This is a distinctive Johannine feature, discerned by Francis Moloney and brilliantly presented throughout his commentary.
8. Moloney, F. J., *op. cit.*, 68.
9. Moloney, F. J., *op. cit.*, 107.
10. Moloney, F. J., *op. cit.*, 148.
11. Harrington W. J., *Matthew: Sage Theologian*, 8-10.
12. Moloney, F. J., *op. cit.*, 223.
13. Moloney, F. J., *op. cit.*, 232.
14. Brodie, Thomas L., *The Gospel According to John. A Literary and Theological Commentary*, (Oxford University Press, 1993), 372.
15. *Op. cit.*, 318f.
16. Moloney, F. J., *op. cit.*, 330f. A parade example of this commentator's striking insights.
17. *Op. cit.*, 384.
18. Brodie, T. L., *op. cit.*, 454.

19. Moloney, F. J., *op. cit.*, 467f.
20. Brown, Raymond E., *The Gospel According to John*, XIII-XXI. (London: G. Chapman, 1971), 843-896.
21. Moloney, F. J., *op. cit.*, 504.
22. Moloney, F. J., op. cit., 527.
23. Moloney, F. J., *op. cit.*, 543.

For Reference and Further Study

JOHN

J. Ashton, *Understanding the Fourth Gospel*, (Oxford: Clarendon Press, 1991).

C. K. Barrett, *The Gospel According to St John*, 2nd ed., (London: SPCK, 1978).

T. L. Brodie, *The Gospel According to John. A Literary and Theological Commentary*, (Oxford: University Press, 1993).

R. E. Brown, *The Gospel According to John*, AB. 2 vols. (Garden City, New York/London: Doubleday/G. Chapman, 1966, 1971).

– 'The Gospel According to John' in *An Introduction to the New Testament*, (New York: Doubleday, 1997), 333-382.

A. T. Hanson, *The Prophetic Gospel*, (Edinburgh: T. & T. Clark, 1991).

J. McPolin, *John*, New Testament Message 6, (Wilmington, DE: M. Glazier, 1979).

F. J. Moloney, *The Gospel of John*, Sacra Pagina 4. A Michael Glazier Book (Collegeville, MN: Liturgical Press, 1998).

R. Schnackenburg, *The Gospel According to St John*, 3 vols. (London/New York: Burns & Oates/Crosssroad, 1968-1982).

Interpretation, 49 (1995), No. 4. *The Gospel of John*.

GENERAL

R. E. Brown, *The Death of the Messiah*, 2 vols. (New York/London: Doubleday/Chapman), 1994).

J. C. Dwyer, *Son of God and Son of Man*, (New York: Paulist,1983).

K. J. Kuschel, *Born Before All Time? The Dispute Over Christ's Origin*, (London: SCM, 1992).

E. Lyons, *Jesus: Self-portrait by God*, (Dublin: The Columba Press, 1994).

J. P. Meier, *A Marginal Jew*, vol. 1. (New York: Doubleday, 1991).

E. P. Sanders, *The Historical Figure of Jesus*, (London: Penguin Books, 1995).

E. Schillebeeckx, *Christ. The Experience of Jesus as Lord*, (New York: Crossroad, 1981).

Index to Johannine Passages

Other titles in this series

Matthew: Sage Theologian
The Jesus of Matthew
Wilfrid J. Harrington OP
ISBN 1 85607 245 2   120 pages   £8.99

Mark: Realistic Theologian
The Jesus of Mark
Wilfrid J. Harrington OP
ISBN 1 85607 169 3   152 pages   £8.99

Luke: Gracious Theologian
The Jesus of Luke
Wilfrid J. Harrington OP
ISBN 1 85607 206 1   120 pages   £8.99

All available from The Columba Press

Also available from Columba

The Jesus Story

Wilfrid J. Harrington OP

Why do we have *four* gospels? After all, Jesus Christ is one person who lived one life. The fact is that none of the evangelists is primarily interested in presenting a biography of Jesus of Nazareth. Each is, in the first place, addressing a Christian community, with the concerns and the needs of that community in mind. His readers knew the basic Jesus story as well as the evangelist. He makes his point by telling the story in *his* way.

This book hits on the novel expedient of having Jesus, the dominant character in each gospel, tell his story in his own words – a story which sounds different in each gospel. The introductory chapter makes clear that the approach, while not aimed at scholars, follows the line of modern scholarly understanding of the gospels.

ISBN 0 948183 93 4   166 pages   £8.99